*for Jacob Burda and Alan Lawson,
in fellowship*

Published by Little Toller Books in 2021

Text © John Burnside 2021

The right of John Burnside to be identified as the author of this work has been asserted by him in accordance with the Copyright, Design and Patents Act 1988

Excerpts from this book have appeared, in abridged form, in *The New Statesman*

Jacket and illustration © Tim Robertson

Typeset in Garamond by Little Toller Books

Printed in Cornwall by TJ Books

All papers used by Little Toller Books are natural, recyclable products made from wood grown in sustainable, well-managed forests

A catalogue record for this book is available from the British Library

All rights reserved

ISBN 978-1-908213-89-1

Aurochs *and* Auks

ESSAYS ON MORTALITY
AND EXTINCTION

JOHN BURNSIDE

LITTLE TOLLER

Contents

Aurochs	7
The hint half guessed, the gift half understood	49
Auks	81
Blossom Ruins	101

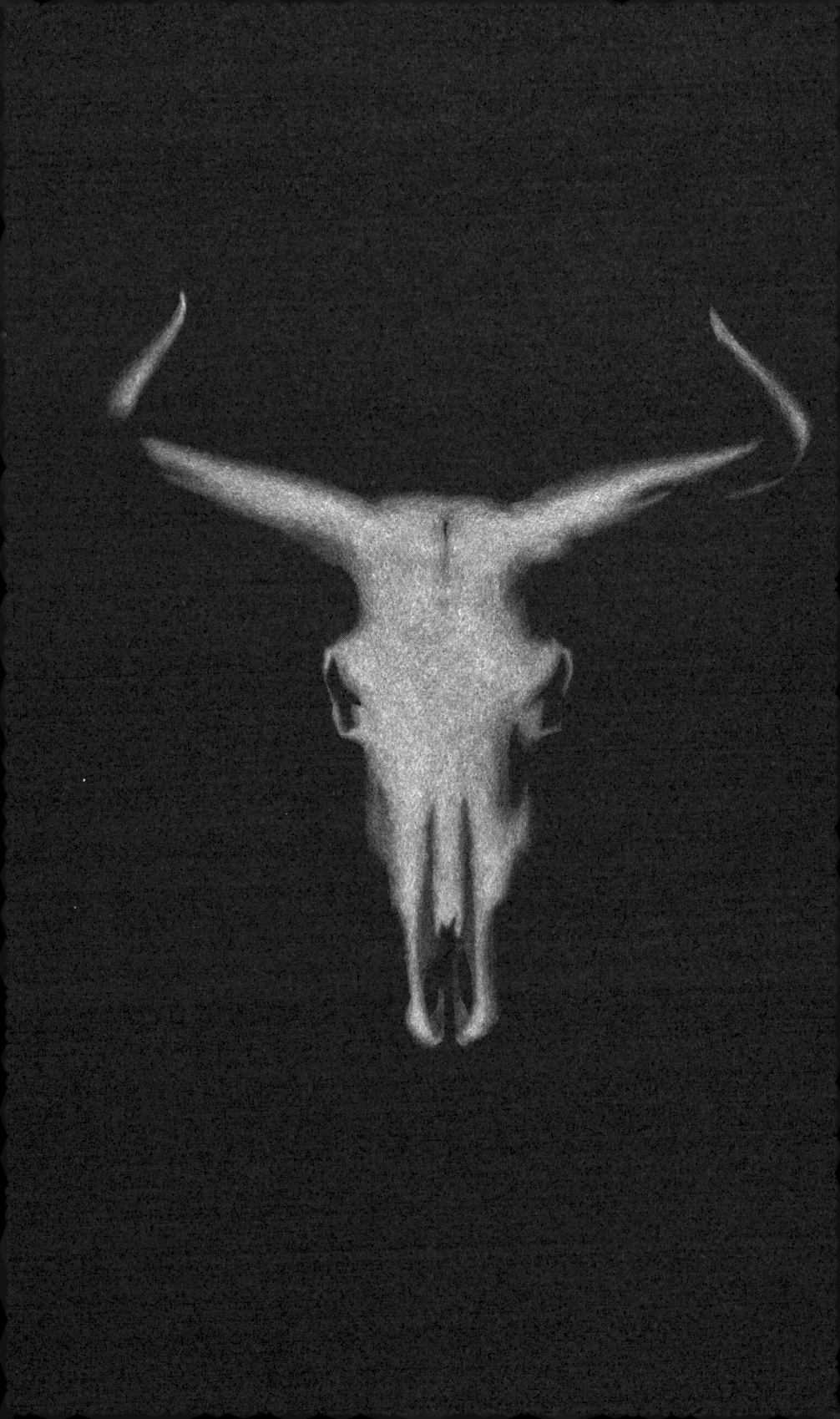

Aurochs

As various as they are in other ways, the common feature of all the stories I have ever loved is some version of the opening line: Once upon a time.

Once upon a time, meaning: not just here or there, in this or that specific location, and not at any determined point in history, but in a realm that is both proximate to this world and, at the same time, wholly *other*. Once upon a time is where the imagination runs free, where stories may be repeated *ad infinitum* and never go stale; originating as it does in a pagan, and so, less reified past, it is the closest thing I have to an aboriginal Dreaming. Once upon a time, things were different: less limited by mere denotation, more fluid. Authorised by no-one and nothing. *Sui generis*. Once upon a time, anything could happen. Birds talked and the more gifted amongst us could understand them. Animals appeared out of nowhere to guide a lost child through the forest. Benevolent shapeshifters wandered the land – and, sometimes, they were us. It was conceivable that linear time might cease, or that one perfect moment might linger indefinitely; it could happen that, merely by stepping over a narrow stream, or passing through a certain gap in a certain hedge, a body might find itself in Tir na Nog.

Once upon a time isn't necessarily confined to prehistory, however. It can unfold in the midst of the banal, flowering out of the Authorised Version of How Things Are (known to the worried adults who raised me as 'The Real World') and transforming what usually belongs to the powers-that-be into an unchartered no-man's land. Charles Dickens conjures up that transformation in the opening of *A Tale of Two Cities:*

> It was the best of times, it was the worst of times, it was the age of wisdom, it was the age of foolishness, it was the epoch of belief, it was the epoch of incredulity, it was the season of Light, it was the season of Darkness, it was the spring of hope, it was the winter of despair, we had everything before us, we had nothing before us, we were all going direct to Heaven, we were all going direct the other way – in short, the period was so far like the present period, that some of its noisiest authorities insisted on its being received, for good or for evil, in the superlative degree of comparison only.

When I first read those lines, I felt a surge of something like gratitude. By then, I had some inkling of how the 'noisiest authorities' worked, and I suspected that Dickens was one of those people who knew, as instinctively as I did, but with more precision of thought, that the *actual*, in all its fleeting beauty and varied textures, had constantly to be rescued from the black and white of The Real World's official report.

I was just as grateful for the opening lines of *Moby Dick*, where Melville has his narrator assume the persona of Ishmael the way an Inuit shaman assumes the mask that permits his spirit to travel in the other world:

> Call me Ishmael. Some years ago – never mind how long precisely – having little or no money in my purse, and nothing particular to interest me on shore, I thought I would sail about a little and see the watery part of the world. It is a way I have of driving off the spleen and regulating the circulation.

This, to me, was the only good reason, not only to go to sea, but to do anything – not for some contingent, entirely practical purpose, but on an impulse, spontaneously, in the spirit of what Ishmael calls 'a choice resulting from my own unbiased freewill and discriminating judgment.' Later, he comes to see this choice as 'a delusion'; but the fact remains that it is *his* delusion, and not some common-sense matter dictated by the orthodoxy of the day – and delusion or not, it unites him with Queequeg, whose transformative power is signalled, not only by the fact that he is 'a native of Rokovoko, an island ... not down on any map' (because, as Melville knows, 'true places never are') but also by his elaborate tattoos:

> the work of a departed prophet and seer ... who,
> by those hieroglyphic marks, had written out on his
> body a complete theory of the heavens and the earth,
> and a mystical treatise on the art of attaining truth;
> so that Queequeg in his own proper person was a
> riddle to unfold; a wondrous work in one volume;
> but whose mysteries not even himself could read,
> though his own live heart beat against them.

These are just two instances where the classic books that my teachers provided not only subverted the conventions by which they would have me live, but also connected me, indirectly, to the Dreaming. However, it was in the fairy tales and myths that I read as a boy that the Dreamtime sparkled and shone most vividly. There, children who were not much different from me passed mysteriously into other worlds and met elfin creatures, or witches, or even the King of the Fairies. There, seal women emerged from the waves to dance on moonlit shores; men became wolves or badgers; girls were transformed into swans. There, the barriers between human and animal were not fixed – and it was this most magical of realms that offered the most radical alternative to authorised history, an Actual to set against the grown-ups' self-designated Reality, a zone teeming with the surprising likenesses and improbable transmogrifications that *once upon a time* makes possible. This is the shadow of the Dreamtime that haunted me then, and lingers with me now, whenever I think about the animals that once lived here and are here no longer. Today, for reasons unforeseen back then, my elders' and betters' 'Real World' so thoroughly occupies me that there is barely room for anything else. In the land of once upon a time, however, a pre-industrial, pre-Anthropocene wildness persists, in stark, green contrast to an occupied planet where human beings and their livestock account for 96 per cent of all living mammals – and it is in this land of once upon a time that the wild bulls of Europe, the aurochs, wandered freely through forest clearings and wetlands for millennia, before they were hunted down, displaced by agricultural enclosure and domesticated into extinction.

The aurochs, wild predecessor of domesticated cattle, originated in India around two million years ago. Gradually, as the climate changed and they migrated westwards into Europe and North Africa, three distinct subspecies emerged, of which the largest (*Bos primigenius*) transformed both the shape and texture, not only of the land (through grazing and foraging) but also of our ancestors' mythmaking. These are the great bulls with elegant lyre-shaped horns and massive, yet surprisingly graceful bodies that we know from the cave paintings at Lascaux and Nerja and Altamira: eerie, yet strangely intimate images, freely depicted in black, red, ochre and deep-brown pigments, around 17,000 BCE, by a people who clearly regarded their subjects with awe and, it would seem, a magical, if not necessarily religious, reverence. Later, when those cave painters had passed from the land, Zeus would take the form of a white aurochs when he abducted Europa, while wild bulls would become central figures in the Cretan rites of spring, where acrobatic young men are shown leaping over the horns of charging bulls in the palace frescoes at Knossos. The Romans placed sacred bulls at the centre of both the Mithras cult and the secret rituals they dedicated to the goddess Cybele, while Pliny the Elder describes the Druidic sacrifice of two white, aurochs-like bulls in Book XVI of his *Natural History*:

> Having made all due preparation for the sacrifice and a banquet beneath the trees, they bring thither two white bulls, the horns of which are bound then for the first time. Clad in a white robe the priest ascends the tree, and cuts the mistletoe with a golden sickle, which is received by others in a white cloak. They then immolate the victims, offering up their prayers that God will render this gift propitious ...[1]

When it comes to the practices of the Celts, we do well to take Classical authors with a pinch of salt: whether from ignorance, or a sense of superiority, or merely for propaganda purposes, they had a tendency to misrepresent the culture and beliefs of those whose lands they had colonised. So it is with all colonists – and it comes as no surprise that Pliny concludes his account with a sardonic coda, in which the implications are clear:

> It is the belief with them that the mistletoe, taken in drink, will impart fecundity to all animals that are barren, and that it is an antidote for all poisons. *Such are the religious feelings which we find entertained towards trifling objects among nearly all nations* [my italics]

---

[1] Pliny the Elder, *The Natural History*, tr. John Bostock and H.T. Riley (1856) Bohn's Classical Library, London.

Likewise, Julius Caesar, a highly effective military propagandist, advances a canny general's image of his erstwhile enemies (in this case, the troublesome Teutons) in the following account of an aurochs encounter from the sixth book of *De Bello Gallico*:

> In size these are somewhat smaller than elephants; in appearance, colour, and shape they are as bulls. Great is their strength and great their speed, and they spare neither man nor beast once sighted. These the Germans slay zealously, by taking them in pits; by such work the young men harden themselves and by this kind of hunting train themselves, and those who have slain most of them bring the horns with them to a public place for a testimony thereof, and win great renown. But even if they are caught very young, the animals cannot be tamed or accustomed to human beings. In bulk, shape and appearance their horns are very different from the horns of our own oxen. The natives collect them zealously and encase the edges with silver, and then at their grandest banquets use them as drinking-cups.[2]

Here, Caesar is pointing out how formidable his German opponents are: that he is able to overcome such wild human creatures in battle is testament to his martial prowess. At the same time, we know that Classical authors were unscientific, at least in modern terms, when it came to natural phenomena: for example, it was Pliny who, following and exaggerating Aristotle, gave the Medieval bestiary the Bonnacon, or Bonasus, a mythical creature, half-bull, half-horse:

> In Pæonia, it is said, there is a wild animal known as the bonasus; it has the mane of the horse, but is, in

2 Caesar: *The Gallic War*, tr. H. J. Edwards (1917) Loeb Classical Library, Harvard University Press.

other respects, like the bull, with horns, however, so much bent inwards upon each other, as to be of no use for the purposes of combat. It has therefore to depend upon its flight, and, while in the act of flying, it sends forth its excrements, sometimes to a distance of even three jugera; the contact of which burns those who pursue the animal, just like a kind of fire.

In the same fanciful spirit, not long before he delivers his account of the aurochs, Caesar offers his readers a wholly unironic anecdote about unicorns. Nevertheless, modern-day palaeontologists believe that his comparison of the aurochs to an elephant is fairly accurate (the elephant to which he refers being a now-extinct North African species that was a little smaller than the elephants we know today). In short, the great bulls that wandered Europe, once upon a time, were much larger than their domesticated and sadly diminished descendants and, for once, Caesar was probably not exaggerating.

Where he is mistaken, though, is in the claim that 'even if they are caught very young, the animals cannot be tamed or accustomed to human beings.' In fact, one of the two main reasons why the aurochs no longer wander Europe today is that they were, in fact, amenable to domestication. Like many species, they were badly impacted by habitat loss due to intensive agriculture, but the other significant factor in their disappearance from the wild is that, as humans moved from hunter-gatherer or nomadic herding practices to permanent occupation of the land, some of the aurochs became the farmed cattle we know today: diminished, bovine in the pejorative sense and, for the most part, almost mechanically utilitarian. In time, as they were enclosed and husbanded in increasing numbers, they developed diseases that they would never have contracted in the forests and wetlands – diseases that quickly spread back to the wild.

It is tempting to speculate as to why civilization began

as it did, and how it managed to succeed. In all likelihood, the new systems of land enclosure and animal appropriation would have met with resistance – evidenced, perhaps, by the Genesis story of Cain and Abel, which tells us that Cain, the farmer slew the herder, Abel, making him the first murderer in human history. For this heinous crime, Cain was driven 'out from the presence of the Lord, and dwelt in the land of Nod, on the east of Eden' – and yet he is the first of Adam's tribe to build a city, which he calls 'after the name of his son, Enoch.' From that first city, a civilization grows. What Abel had represented was the old, nomadic way of life, where smallish groups of humans followed herds and flocks of semi-wild beasts, living alongside them, taking only what they needed to sustain themselves. The children of Cain, however, are *developers*. 'Artificers in brass and iron,' creators of enclosures and fixed abodes, they unrelentingly wield the plough, never spare the rod and, with the passing of the ages, address themselves to the godlike task of domesticating all wild things, including their own imaginations. The children of Cain are warlike and unforgiving: any perceived aggressor is met with savage and disproportionate force ('If Cain shall be avenged sevenfold, truly Lamech seventy and sevenfold' says Genesis 4:24). Cain's ilk destroys natural habitats; their livestock spread disease to the wandering beasts that the herders follow, they invent the laws that put property before life. Eventually, the wilderness dwindles to nothing, as his descendants enclose and overgraze what remains of the earth – until, at last, they go global, clear-felling great forests for timber decking and hardwood chopsticks, slaughtering vast herds of buffalo from slow-moving trains and over-fishing the oceans to the point of exhaustion. And as they go, they leave behind them a long trail of extinctions, of which the loss of the aurochs is only one of many.

★

There is a poem by the American poet, Lucie Brock-Broido, that begins:

> The extinct creatures would have liked this day,
> a festival flooded all the way to the river.³

As always with Brock-Broido, the poem works on a number of levels, but the immediate effect of these opening lines is to create a sense of kinship with those extinct animals, as they experience the kind of pleasure that the poet, or the reader, might enjoy on a fine autumn day, delighting in the quotidian contentment of:

> the love of old leaves heaped,
> the dogs barking down
> the late afternoons, howling for summertime.

As the poem continues, Brock-Broido weaves in human subjects, including Anne Boleyn – the innocent victim at the centre of a cynical political drama in which:

> An entire country
> changed its faith once for its king

– as well as some 'invalids... whorled in white coverlets', who gradually become 'exhausted from yearning', while weathering changes that they cannot control. It is clear, however, that these more recent human subjects live in a world that is painfully diminished by comparison with that of their extinct predecessors:

> Everything they do is smaller than these
> who walked in a world
> that is greener than this one.

---

3 'Evolution' from Lucy Brock-Broido, *A Hunger*, Knopf, New York, 1988.

With this simple, yet effective re-animation of green-as-metaphor, the poet adds a hint of nostalgia to her portrayal of the extinct creatures – a nostalgia that the reader, who has never experienced that original green world, can only share vicariously – and as she does so, she creates a sympathetic parallel between humans and the creatures we have replaced. *They* would have enjoyed the sense of festival that this flooded day brings, just as we, it is implied, experience a proxy regret for a world that once was greener than our own. So it is that, as strange and as distant in time and place as we and those creatures are, our commonality – the commonality of all living creatures – is made apparent, even as the poet refuses to succumb to the usual nature-writing clichés.

Of course, it would be easy to argue that Brock-Broido's stance here is presumptuous. None of us can speak with any confidence about the few animals that we encounter day-to-day (our pets, our livestock, the odd deer glimpsed through a windshield), never mind the extinct creatures of these opening lines. Thoroughly tamed, sadly domesticated and locked into the virtual, we can only guess what an extinct animal might experience, were it to fetch up in the modern world – and, of course, Brock-Broido knows this. In fact, it is the presumption that makes this poem so powerful, for it is the same presumption that sits at the heart of all communal life. We have to *imagine* what others are feeling and we can never be sure that we have guessed aright, as Wittgenstein points out in his now-notorious 'beetle in the box' analogy[4]:

> Suppose everyone had a box with something in it: we call it a 'beetle'. No one can look into anyone else's box, and everyone says he knows what a beetle is only by looking at his beetle. Here it would be quite possible for everyone to have something different

---

4 Ludwig Wittgenstein: *Philosophical Investigations*, tr. G. E. M. Ancombe (1953) Basil Blackwell Ltd, London.

in his box. One might even imagine such a thing constantly changing.

In purely rational terms, this is undeniably the case. Even amongst creatures of the same species, working with a shared language, there can be no assured knowledge of another's experiences. This is, in fact, a truism. Empathy, sympathy, connection of any kind, is mostly based on intuition, not deductive logic. Guesswork. As we grow older, some of us refine that intuitive sense of the other's subjectivity, while others abandon it altogether. But for as long as we live, we can never be *rationally* certain that we understand, or even share, the same imaginative or emotional climate as others. And such a presumption of *une vie commune* is even greater when it comes to other species, especially species that died out centuries ago.[5]

---

5 I have borrowed the term 'une vie commune' from a specific usage in the collaborationist French writer Jacques Chardonne's book, *L'amour c'est beaucoup plus que l'amour* (Editions Albin Michel, Paris, 1957) specifically in the passage:

> *Ce n'est pas le premier amour qui compte, ni le second, ni le dernier. C'est celui qui a mêlé deux destinées dans la vie commune.* [It is not the first love that matters, nor the second, nor the last. It is the one that has mingled two destinies in communal life.]

Clearly, Chardonne's view is of a specific human community, with its own very specific customs and mores. For present purposes, however, this is only a starting point; drawing, first, on the philosophy of Emmanuel Levinas, whose work demands that such commonality must be extended to all humans, and second, on ideas from Asian thought (summed up in the Buddhist call to compassion for all sentient beings) and from deep ecology, I want to propose that the notion of *une vie commune*, as a theatre of interanimation, applies not only to *Homo sapiens* (as in, say, C.G. Jung's concept of a collective unconscious) but to all life as such. The contention is simply that, because all life is predicated on a symbiotic continuum, all individual lives are governed by a common destiny – a natural fact that we must learn, not just to recognise, but to set at the heart of our ethics, our politics, and our day-to-day lives, if we are to avoid a human extinction. In short, the most mature, the most fully developed and, indeed, the inevitable practice of *une vie commune* is to be found in a lived, deliberate conviviality, in which all life is *felt* to be continuous.

But then, this is exactly the point. All connection, all fellow feeling, is an exercise in imagination: what we know of other lives, beyond the superficial, depends upon intuition and empathy – and upon what the Spanish poet-philosopher Maria Zambrano calls *la razón poética*. Under the aegis of our present 'hard-science' orthodoxy, the main problem, when speaking of this poetic reasoning aloud, is the notion, advanced by some in this strictly orthodox camp, that those who espouse poetic reasoning want to do away with logic altogether, to base everything on fancy and vague, touchy-feely, New-Age sentiment. But this is not the case at all – and it is always surprising when anyone takes such arguments seriously. The great gift of having a human, rather than a mechanical mind is that it combines many faculties, whether deductive, affective, imaginative or spontaneously intuitive (improvisatory), and it is pure foolishness to limit these many gifts to favour just one. If you insist on a kind of blanket objectivity – if, as a matter of orthodoxy, you set aside imagination, intuition and all the other unquantifiable faculties that human bodies possess – then, of course, there is no way that a contemporary American poet can know what the extinct animals would have liked. But, by the same token, you would also be obliged to declare Keats' 'Ode on a Grecian Urn' a series of fanciful generalisations concluding with the tautology: 'Beauty is truth, truth beauty', while Wallace Stevens' inexplicably powerful declaration, in 'Thirteen Ways of Looking at a Blackbird':

> A man and a woman
> Are one.
> A man and a woman and a blackbird
> Are one.

would have to be dismissed as frivolous. Objectively, only a very few poems make any kind of conventional sense at all;

but then, *objectively*, any notion of a shared reality, beyond the basic fabric of matter and atmosphere, remains unprovable. Using objective methods, we can *describe* the morphology and (outward) behaviour of other living creatures quite well, but we can only *know* them – provisionally, tentatively – by using *all* of our faculties, including intuition and empathy. Sadly, since the beginning of the Industrial Revolution, those who manage the world have decreed that only what is objective (testable, measurable, bottom line) can be considered relevant in the new orthodoxy. This has led to a functional, utilitarian approach to everything, especially 'Nature': ever since the first Gradgrindly victories of nineteenth-century entrepreneurship, any publicly maintained vision of the world we inhabit is of an agglomeration of workable land and exploitable resources. It is this vision that once prompted Ronald Reagan to say:

> I think, too, that we've got to recognize that where the preservation of a natural resource like the redwoods is concerned, that there is a common sense limit. I mean, if you've looked at a hundred thousand acres or so of trees – you know, a tree is a tree, how many more do you need to look at? [sic]

The answer, of course, should have been evident, even to a man like Reagan. A tree is, indeed, a tree, and a forest is a forest. But these two are quite different phenomena – and when we become so 'objective' that we can no longer see the forest for the trees, or the trees for the forest, we leave the world vulnerable to new forms of extinction. Even Julius Caesar and his fellow conquerors, who often had to learn about forests the hard way, could have told us that much.

★

Just as we cannot say how the extinct creatures would have felt about today's world, so we cannot know what the artists who made the Lascaux or Altamira cave paintings felt about the animals they depicted so vividly in their work. We cannot understand how it felt for them to move amongst the other creatures, exposed to predators as they broke cover to cross open spaces or ford wide, fast-flowing rivers, constantly on guard against a chance encounter with something heavy and powerful that, even if it had no desire to eat them, might take umbrage at their presence and gore, crush, or trample them to death. Anyone who has ever worked with modern-day cattle knows how risky it can be to get between, say, a Holstein and her calf: imagine the danger of finding oneself caught out in the space between an infant aurochs and a full-grown bull – an animal of around a ton in weight and equipped with horns of up to thirty-inches in length. It would be naïve, then, to discount fear as a factor in the animal encounters of our Palaeolithic ancestors. On the other hand, that fear may well have been mitigated by an increase in self-awareness, an intimation, perhaps, of needful humility, accompanied by a growing sense of humour about the human predicament. As Barbara Ehrenreich points out[6]:

> Our ancestors occupied a lowly spot in the food chain, at least compared to the megafauna, but at the same time they were capable of understanding and depicting how lowly it was. They knew they were meat, and they also seemed to know that they knew they were meat – meat that could think. And that, if you think about it long enough, is almost funny…

and she adds that we should study Palaeolithic art works:

---

6   Barbara Ehrenreich: 'Humans were not centre stage: how ancient cave art puts us in our place', *The Baffler* magazine, November 2019.

not just because they are still capable of inspiring transcendent experiences and connecting us with the long-lost natural world. We should be drawn back to them for the message they have reliably preserved for more than 10,000 generations ... because our Palaeolithic ancestors, with their faceless humanoids and capacity for silliness, seem to have known something we strain to imagine. They knew where they stood in the scheme of things, which was not very high, and this seems to have made them laugh. I strongly suspect that we will not survive the mass extinction we have prepared for ourselves unless we too finally get the joke.[7]

I like this argument. It pleases me, and so, I find it persuasive. At the same time, however, it does not exclude the possibility of a certain non-religious, or at least unorthodox reverence, or some kind of creaturely affinity. After all, it would be as reductive to assume that cosmic laughter and reverence are mutually exclusive as it is to assume, with the reductionists themselves, that the only mental faculty that we can trust is objective reasoning.

That said, I happily admit that the reverential quality I find in cave paintings is wholly subjective. I have no way of knowing what Palaeolithic artists felt about their subjects, whether they were creating a visual focus or totem to assist them in hunting, or invoking a spirit of some kind as a means to exploring altered states of consciousness, or even simply scrawling graffiti on the nearest available surface to pass the time and amuse their kin. This last option seems less likely when we consider the lengths to which they must have gone,

---

7 ibid.

in order to mine the necessary pigments and other materials – but there really is no need to presume on this, or any other evidence to make the case. I have no problem admitting that reverence is a feeling that the cave paintings prompt me to discover in myself and, so, by extension, in the minds of those who created them. But then, this is how all art operates. The creator of a piece can explain at length why he or she made it – witness the many artists' statements supplied by galleries and exhibition catalogues, especially for those works considered conceptual in nature – but if I do not feel it, there is not much point in a formal explanation. It's like explaining a joke, or trying to justify cosmic laughter, for that matter: either you get it, or you don't and, if you do get it, then cave art needs no explaining. It provokes a series of responses, one of which is an appreciation of how freely the figures are drawn, while another might be an aesthetic response to the use of colour to create a world. Yet another might be a sense of reverence. Awe. An intuition that, in spirit, we are with people who felt the sacredness of being for its own sake. The fact of presence. The improbable truth that, through an unlikely series of coincidences, from the exact tilt of the planet on its axis to various shifts in weather and atmosphere, life happens here, on Earth. When we choose to speak of such things, we may be taking various caveats as given, but then, all speech is a risk, and an effort, just as all listening is an effort. An effort, and a responsibility. And when we *do* speak of such matters, in so many words, a well-entrenched orthodoxy is there to dismiss the argument as being fanciful, subjective and, because it cannot be quantified, scientifically invalid. A fit subject for poetry, no doubt, but no part of any grown-up, societal, Real World discussion.

In her essay on Palaeolithic art, Barbara Ehrenreich says, *en passant*, that when the paintings were made, their authors could not have imagined 'such perverse and self-destructive descendants as we have become' – and she is not exaggerating. Perverse destruction, driven by objective, bottom-line, profit-and-loss motives remains the societal norm, in spite of the ubiquitous 'green' rhetoric that peppers, but never quite transforms public discourse. There was a time when it was possible to imagine that, as species loss and environmental degradation became progressively more acute, more people would not only notice what was going on but change the way they lived. And, in fact, considerable numbers of those who can afford it are now making adjustments – though these are minor, insufficient and, at times, entirely gestural. What we seem unprepared to accept, however, are the *real* changes that must take place in order to end, or at least slow, the destruction – and every day, more species are lost while, with fateful irony, the world we have consistently refused to share with our wild neighbours grows more and more inimical to an increasingly perilous human enterprise.

Après nous, le déluge, then. But first, a story. A children's story, in fact, from over a hundred years ago when, as industrial grade as modern life had already become, almost nobody believed that the land was beyond saving.

Kenneth Grahame published *The Wind in the Willows* in 1908. It is the tale of a lovable Mole and his friends – a Rat, a Badger, a family of Otters and the technology-fixated Toad of Toad Hall, whose obsession with powerful motor cars leads to theft, public ignominy and a farcical court appearance, at the end of which he is sentenced to twenty years in 'the remotest dungeon of the best-guarded keep of the stoutest castle in all the length and breadth of Merry England', in part for stealing the car and endangering public safety, but mostly for 'cheeking the police.' Like so many books that are now classified as children's literature, *The Wind in the Willows* is a mix of dark humour, social satire and touching, but far from sentimentalised, encounters between the various friends (the rescue of Little Portly, the Otter child, is particularly affecting). For present purposes, however, I want to concentrate on a single chapter, one that is often overlooked and is certainly under-appreciated. That chapter is 'The Piper at the Gates of Dawn', in which, at that moment of the day when darkness gradually turns to light, and the border between the quotidian world and whatever realm it is that lies beyond is at its thinnest, the Mole and the Rat encounter a mysterious, elemental being, whose identity is never stated in so many words. No need to say that *The Wind in the Willows* belongs very firmly to the highest echelon of once upon a time narratives, but this chapter is special, even in that context, a kind of heightened once upon a time interlude within the larger once upon a time of the novel. Here, we find only as much of the English Dreamtime as remained to its suburbanised citizens in the early 1900s, but it is as magical, in its way, as any tale from the mists of Faerie.

Fittingly enough, this entry to the Dreaming begins at moonrise. Not yet ready to sleep, Mole and Rat take their little rowboat for a paddle upstream, moving out into the middle of the river to follow a 'clear, narrow track that faintly reflected the sky', away from the treacherous shadows of the tree-lined bank. Almost immediately, their surroundings are transformed:

> over the rim of the waiting earth the moon lifted with slow majesty till it swung clear of the horizon and rode off, free of moorings; and once more they began to see surfaces – meadows widespread, and quiet gardens, and the river itself from bank to bank, all softly disclosed, all washed clean of mystery

and terror, all radiant again as by day, but with a difference that was tremendous. Their old haunts greeted them again in other raiment, as if they had slipped away and put on this pure new apparel and come quietly back ...[8]

This is where the other world begins, not on the far side of some supernatural borderline, but here, in the landscape that they know and take for granted, their old haunts *softly disclosed* by nothing more than a shift in the light. Almost as soon as they have entered this softly disclosed night-time world, the Rat begins to hear a far and elusive piping, a music that he has 'never dreamed ... and the call in it is stronger even than the music is sweet.' To begin with, Mole hears nothing more than 'the wind playing in the reeds and rushes and osiers', but after a moment, as they come closer to its source, the glad piping breaks on him 'like a wave' and, 'possessed' by the strange music, he rows harder towards it, until the two animals come to a great weir, in the midst of which a small island lies 'anchored', concealing 'whatever it might hold behind a veil, keeping it till the hour should come, and, with the hour, those who were called and chosen.' It is here, in the place that the Rat calls 'the place of my song-dream, the place the music played to me', that the two friends finally reach the source of the piping that had drawn them onward, and the Mole is vouchsafed, first a premonition, and then a vision of a being that, as much as it resembles Pan, or one of the old Celtic horned gods, is named only as 'the Friend and Helper':

> Then suddenly the Mole felt a great Awe fall upon him, an awe that turned his muscles to water, bowed his head, and rooted his feet to the ground. It was no panic terror – indeed he felt wonderfully at peace

---

8 Kenneth Grahame, *The Wind in the Willows*, Methuen, London, 1908.

and happy – but it was an awe that smote and held
him and, without seeing, he knew it could only
mean that some august Presence was very, very near.
With difficulty he turned to look for his friend, and
saw him at his side, cowed, stricken, and trembling
violently. And still there was utter silence in the
populous bird-haunted branches around them; and
still the light grew and grew.⁹

And the vision continues:

Perhaps he would never have dared to raise his
eyes, but that, though the piping was now hushed,
the call and the summons seemed still dominant
and imperious. He might not refuse, were Death
himself waiting to strike him instantly, once he
had looked with mortal eye on things rightly
kept hidden. Trembling he obeyed, and raised his
humble head; and then, in that utter clearness of the
imminent dawn, while Nature, flushed with fulness
of incredible colour, seemed to hold her breath for
the event, he looked in the very eyes of the Friend
and Helper; saw the backward sweep of the curved
horns, gleaming in the growing daylight; saw the
stern, hooked nose between the kindly eyes that
were looking down on them humorously, while the
bearded mouth broke into a half-smile at the corners;
saw the rippling muscles on the arm that lay across
the broad chest, the long supple hand still holding
the pan-pipes only just fallen away from the parted
lips; saw the splendid curves of the shaggy limbs
disposed in majestic ease on the sward ...¹⁰

Now, having come face to face with a living, muscular,
hirsute embodiment of the Natural Sublime, the diminutive

9   ibid
10 ibid

friends lapse, for a moment, into self-consciousness, and Mole asks the Rat if he is afraid:

> 'Afraid?' murmured the Rat, his eyes shining with unutterable love. 'Afraid? Of Him? O, never, never! And yet – and yet – O, Mole, I am afraid.'[11]

Rarely has there been such a clear and vivid description of the encounter with the Sublime – and it is told in such a way that any child can, not so much understand as *feel* that moment with the two animal protagonists. I can only speak for myself now, but I suspect that many children have found this passage heartening and affirmative over the years, just as I did when I first read it. For, like many children, I had experienced moments of mixed love and fear that did not accord with – that could not be accommodated by – the Authorised Version that my elders and betters had to offer. This chapter gave me permission not to dismiss out of hand those moments of apprehension and awe that I had experienced from time to time out in the woods around our prefab, or on some borderline between worlds that I had stumbled across in the neighbouring fields. I am not talking about 'the supernatural' here, and I did not see my encounters with the Friend and Helper as religious, or even spiritual. They were part and parcel of being alive, of being *here*. One presence in a continuum of presences and, so, a constituent of the Overall that A.R. Ammons characterises as being both 'beyond me' and, at the same time, subject to apprehension as:

> the sum of these events
> I cannot draw, the ledger I cannot keep, the accounting
> beyond the account:[12]

---

[11] ibid

[12] A.R. Ammons: 'Corson's Inlet', in *Collected Poems 1951–1971*, W.W. Norton, 2001.

Awe. The Natural Sublime. The Overall. These are just words, of course. After the vision, after the encounter, the image of the demiurge fades away, till nothing is left but a vague sense of having heard or seen something – and for mortals, this is a mercy:

> For this is the last best gift that the kindly demi-god is careful to bestow on those to whom he has revealed himself in their helping: the gift of forgetfulness. Lest the awful remembrance should remain and grow, and overshadow mirth and pleasure, and the great haunting memory should spoil all the after-lives of little animals helped out of difficulties, in order that they should be happy and light-hearted as before.
>
> Mole rubbed his eyes and stared at Rat, who was looking about him in a puzzled sort of way. 'I beg your pardon; what did you say, Rat?' he asked.[13]

Rat returns to the quotidian world immediately the vision is passed, and in doing so, discovers the lost otter-child, Portly. However, his companion is slower to recover his composure:

> But Mole stood still a moment, held in thought. As one wakened suddenly from a beautiful dream, who struggles to recall it, and can recapture nothing but a dim sense of the beauty of it, the beauty! Till that, too, fades away in its turn, and the dreamer bitterly accepts the hard, cold waking and all its penalties; so Mole, after struggling with his memory for a brief space, shook his head sadly and followed the Rat.[14]

We do not need to understand the Overall; it is enough to know that it is there. After the holy encounter, we must return

---

13 Grahame op cit.
14 ibid

to the quotidian – for this is where we belong – but we go back with a sense of something, not so much understood, as apprehended. A sense of the mystery of being, of incarnation. We have no proof, no evidence of the kingdom at hand – but there are traces, signs, tracks that cannot be explained away by those who have not stood in the midst of wildness:

> The Mole ran quickly to comfort the little animal; but Rat, lingering, looked long and doubtfully at certain hoof-marks deep in the sward.
> 'Some – great – animal – has been here,' he murmured slowly and thoughtfully; and stood musing, musing; his mind strangely stirred.[15]

Returning from this encounter, we are neither exalted nor demeaned – but some vague sense of kinship may be confirmed. We feel more creaturely. We feel that we belong.

As the cave-painters would have known, it is absurd for thinking meat to feel exalted – and as Ehrenreich tells it, they countered such impulses with cosmic laughter. By contrast, the oft-cited sensation of being diminished by the Sublime – a response too often mistaken for humility – is more of a problem. In truth, I have always been troubled when people say that they feel 'small' or 'insignificant' in their encounters with Grandeur. It would be fine, I suppose, if such encounters really did lead to humility, but I am cautious of those who, feeling belittled by the presence of something larger, succumb to the temptation, sometimes unwittingly, of puffing themselves up and becoming *big*. History has taught us that few things are as dangerous as a

[15] ibid

human being smitten with a sense of personal inadequacy. A great deal of our 'perverse and self-destructive behaviour', from the accumulation of riches that one cannot use to all-out species destruction, arises as a consequence of a severe inferiority complex. And yet, if the wild, if the sublime, if the fleeting encounter with Pan teaches us anything, it is that being here is a matter of scale and of the unique perspective that scale allows. Out in the wild, or gazing up at the stars, lost in the tundra or walking in the desert, meeting an Arctic Fox on the snowy Finnmarksvidda or coming upon fresh bear scat on a hiking trail in British Columbia, I do not feel diminished. On the contrary, I feel appropriate, one instance of a particular species with its own way of being in the world, its own sensory apparatus, its own individual awareness. Every meeting with vastness that has been given to me to witness (a night-sky teeming with stars above the Argentine pampas, say, or the Atlantic Ocean seen from the very tip of Skellig Michael, just twelve miles off the Irish coast) has only confirmed my sense of creatureliness, of being here, amongst all the other living things, and making the best sense I can of it all in my own idiom, even while wishing that I could stop time just long enough to grasp what keeps sliding away – what, in spite of its intensity, will be forgotten, in its essence, as thoroughly as the Mole forgets his vision of The Dawn Piper. The greatest blessing, however, comes from accepting that, from where I stand, I must settle for a regimen of fleeting impressions and privileged glimpses, because I am mortal. This is what it is to be meat that can think: a lifetime of hints and guesses, or rather, *pace* the T.S. Eliot of 'The Dry Salvages', *hints half guessed, and gifts half understood.* Yet, even in this half-knowing, more or less provisional condition, I am able to feel that I belong. Meat that can think, far from grand but quietly to scale, I *participate*. Eliot calls this Incarnation, George Seferis sees it as *the common miracle,* Walt Whitman uncovers it everywhere he goes, in the animals with whom he feels a shared wildness – *I too am not a bit tamed*, he says, *I too am untranslatable* – and in the people he passes by 'each singing what belongs to him or her and to none else.'

Some years ago, I lived with a farmer's daughter from Gloucestershire. Our day-to-day life was strictly suburban – she was a lecturer, I worked in computer systems – but every month or so we would pass a long weekend on the family farm, not far from Stroud, where her father kept cattle and sheep. Up to that point, livestock had been little more than furniture to me: I would meet herds of cattle on country walks, or find them standing in a yard in winter, one great, undifferentiated mass of flesh and steam, and I would feel slightly discomfited, touched with the same unease that I had felt on visits to the zoo as a boy, guilty like a thief, though what it was that had been stolen was difficult to define. There was no sign of obvious cruelty, or at least, not of the kind that I had seen applied to beasts of burden on my various travels, and none of these animals was visibly suffering, like the rabbits I had stumbled upon while working at a field station in Cambridge some years earlier, an encounter that provoked what must be glossed over here as a renewed engagement with animal rights. (I had been hired to assist in the breeding of insects for various research programmes, but nobody had told me about the experiments being conducted in one particular building, the only one for which I normally did not hold a key. There, as I discovered through a mix of carelessness on the part of my boss and native curiosity, subject animals were strapped to boards, then exposed to disease-bearing parasites, for reasons that I chose not to pursue at the time.) By comparison with those rabbits, the cattle on that Gloucestershire farm were treated quite well, albeit on their way to the stun gun, or the knacker's yard. Nevertheless, even on idyllic summer walks amongst a herd of grazing Friesians, or passing through the dairy at milking time, I always felt uncomfortable. I could never put my finger on it, but I was aware of a vague dismay, an undefined sense of loss.

On those monthly trips to the farm, I was expected to put aside such effete ponderings and help out from time to time. I learned how to walk across a field with the necessary air of deliberation, making vague guttural noises that, for the most part, the cattle took in good heart, allowing themselves to be driven back to the yard, or to another field, with minimal resistance. I even learned how to stand my ground when Henry, the Hereford bull, decided he wasn't budging, and turned to gaze at me with his big sad eyes, testing my resolve, doling out a minor reality check as I went about a business that he knew wasn't really mine. After one mildly disquieting incident, I took careful note of the old farmer's advice and made sure I did not position myself between a cow and her calf and, after a while, I began to feel less put-upon when somebody asked me to help bring in the cows. I will not say I enjoyed the work, but it was preferable to dealing with the sheep, who occupied their own, wholly alternative world, one where I was inadmissible, even as a bystander.

That said, there were two occasions when I was almost overwhelmed by my soft-heartedness towards what the old farmer called his 'beasts.' The first was on the night after a batch of calves were taken from their mothers and sent to market. This was an experience I was to have several times, an experience to which, I am sorry to admit, I eventually grew accustomed, but that first night was piteous. When I stayed on the farm, I slept in a cosy first-floor room at the far end of the hall, overlooking the yard. One of the luxuries of the countryside, for me, was that I could sleep with my windows wide open – a pleasure that, after a burglary back home in Surrey, I usually had to forego – and so, that night as always, I had raised the sash several inches, to let the cool air circulate while I lay reading (this was very much an early to bed, early to rise family, and we rarely stayed up past nine o'clock). On that first market night, however, it was impossible to read – and all through, not only that night, but the day and night that followed, I got little rest, even with the windows tightly closed, as the cows gave voice to their dismay and pain, a plaint so mournful that, in the end, I was obliged to go out and follow a dark, narrow lane down to the village, where I sat in the churchyard for an hour, soaking up the quiet. At that time, the accepted wisdom, in rural communities at least, was that farm animals are not encumbered with the awkward emotional baggage that humans carry – and by that token, they were immune to such feelings as attachment or grief. True, a cow sometimes bawled a little when her calf was taken away, but that was just instinct. Maybe this was so; but that night, and on the days that followed, the grief those cattle were feeling seemed to me not much different from the grief a human subject might experience on being parted with a loved one. This was not a view I was inclined to express in company, however; in the rural community, there are few sins as reprehensible as sentimentality about the beasts.

My most disquieting experience with the bovine mind, however, came during a Christmas holiday that I had reluctantly agreed to spend on the farm. I had dearly wished and had even started making plans to go elsewhere but, in spite of the fact that I had never once been greeted by my partner's family with anything that might have been mistaken for warmth or, worse, enthusiasm, I had somehow yielded to the argument that, if I did stay away, everyone would be *deeply disappointed*. I sincerely doubted this, but

I have never been very good at putting my foot down and, as soon as I could reasonably get off work, she and I drove down to Gloucestershire, where we found the farmhouse buried in snow and the windows lit pale-gold against the late-afternoon dusk, like a scene from an old Christmas card. Indoors, my partner's mother was decking the rooms with the holly she had cut from one of several trees in the garden, and the air was thick with the mixed aromas of newly baked bread and traditional winter broth. For a moment, the interior looked like the set in some old British film from the 1950s, a throwback to a time when the word *idyll* could be spoken without irony – and then the old farmer came in, his overalls spattered with muck and engine oil, followed by my partner's brother who, according to some law of nature that applies only in rural communities, appeared to be even older, in his manner and speech, than the old farmer himself. The two men nodded in my direction, emitted the single grunt that was their usual greeting, and plumped into chairs, where they sat waiting for their tea to be brought in the crude greenish crockery that they always used, disdaining the finer bone china that the woman of the house would occasionally attempt to bring out for special occasions. Feeling called upon to be polite, I enquired as to the state of things on the farm and remarked in passing on the unusually deep snow on the roads. To this, the old farmer responded with a flurry of grunts that sounded vaguely agreeable, though agreeable to what, I could not say. After that, neither spoke to me again directly until two days later, when I was required to help out with one of the cows, who had gone down with milk fever.

As idyllic as it was, especially in the springtime, when long chains of purple aubretias cascaded over the limestone walls, or on summer mornings, when swallows flitted back and forth from the main house to the low, stone-built dairy, I never felt altogether *right* in that house. This had to do, no doubt, with a persistent suspicion that, in spite of the agreeable grunts, I was decidedly *persona non grata* with the old farmer and his son, who had preferred my partner's previous beau, a highly practical book-shy type from good farming stock. To them, I was a city boy with an interest in suspect literature and even more suspect politics. In that corner of the world, as in so many other corners of England, a man thought, did and – most particularly – voted as his father had done, which usually meant casting his ballot for the son of a well-to-do landowner or some retired military specimen. Conservative, of course. At my partner's urging, I had been careful never to talk about politics on the farm, but it seems that, as soon as they met me, the entire family had concluded that I was, beyond a doubt, *Labour*. I can only imagine what would have transpired had they known my true affiliations.

All of these were issues that we contrived to work around, but there was something else about the place that troubled me. I had felt it on other farms too, when I was obliged to go visiting – a vague unease, a sense that, even while those who lived there owned and worked the place, they didn't really belong. Something else was in the house, something that had preceded them and wasn't altogether ready to grant them living space. It was no more than a vague, close to subliminal unease that they felt, but I was certain that they felt it, nonetheless. Of course, everyone told ghost stories, but that was tongue-in-cheek, to amuse outsiders and children; they didn't really believe. And yet, they did seem to be haunted by some presence or psychic weather for which they had no words. Maybe they felt there was some knowledge that they lacked, or some ceremony that they had failed to perform, a magic ritual whose omission excluded them from full occupancy. Maybe it was a dearth of cat or heron bones behind the chimney breast. Perhaps they knew, at some level, that they were ignorant of an antique wisdom that the old folk had observed, building something animate into the fabric of the place so that the house could be properly guarded against itself; perhaps they simply lacked the sense of entitlement that allowed their more powerful neighbours to swan around the village like they owned the place. Which they did, of course.

Still, whatever the reason, I never felt that the old farmer was altogether comfortable in his own house. Which was odd because, at such times as he did grace the indoors with his presence, he was its undisputed lord and master, exercising total dominion over a unique throne-like chair in which nobody else was allowed to sit, as well as complete mastery of the television remote, which he used, not only to select his preferred programmes (the horse racing, *Farming Today*) but also to impose a soundscape on the kitchen space that, being partly deaf, he possibly didn't realise was a torment to others.

Still, this power notwithstanding, the old man never seemed fully at ease – and the unexpected consequence of his discomfort was that, whenever we were out of doors, he softened a little towards me. Not enough to engage in anything but the most desultory of exchanges (at times I suspected that the old farmer had never had a full-scale conversation with anyone in his life) but enough that I didn't feel quite so much of an intruder in his world. To him, I am sure, everything I did to help was executed in the most cack-handed manner, but I think he appreciated the fact that I was prepared to get my hands dirty and muck in. He never asked for help directly, but on those occasions when my partner nagged me to go out and lend a hand, he would accept some degree of assistance, as long as it was purely manual. Anything skilled, of course, would have been beyond me – on that we all tacitly agreed. That day, however (which, as it happened, was Christmas Eve) I was permitted a fleeting glimpse of his world, when he led me across the snowy yard to where one of the cows, a huge, sad-looking Friesian, stood in the middle of a small, enclosed space, wobbling and swaying like a house of cards in a sudden draught, her head swinging slowly towards us as we approached, though it quickly became clear that this was as much movement as she could manage on her own. And then, as if to prove that point, her legs crumpled, and she fell, folding, concertina-like, on to the concrete floor.

'We have to get her up, and keep her on her feet,' the old farmer said. This was the most intelligible thing he had ever said to me, in all the time we had known one another.

I felt a surge of scepticism running through me. How the hell were we, an old man and an incompetent, going to achieve such a miracle? It seemed altogether unlikely: and yet, raise her we did, so that she managed to stand for a time, quivering and swaying but making not a single sound – until, all at once, she fell again, so abruptly as she had done before, in fact, that it was like watching an action replay. At this, the old farmer gestured vaguely to me, and we began to raise her again – and then, when she fell yet again, to raise her once more, until, for one long moment of seeming success, she seemed capable of standing by herself, lifting her head a little and gazing at the old man with something like hope in her eyes. Feeling heartened by this, I also turned to him, awaiting further instruction – and this was when the cow chose to fall again, not directly, but just slightly hefting to one side. My side.

I am not sure, now, what I saw, or how I knew she was falling in my direction, but I must have sensed *something*, because at that very moment I stepped back. Not enough to move clear of the falling beast, but enough, nevertheless, that no bones were broken. Had I remained still, she would have taken me down with her, probably crushing my pelvis, or breaking my thigh bones at the very least. As it happened, however, the backward step I had taken meant that she fell on to my lower legs, trapping me against the concrete floor, but doing no real damage. By some fluke, I had stepped back and turned slightly, which meant that, as I hit the ground, my head took a knock but, the fact that I was now trapped under what felt like a dead weight notwithstanding, my luck had held.

That was when I looked – really looked – into the face of the cow for the first time. I had noticed her expression before, I had sensed the mix of hope and dismay she had shown at the old farmer's approach, but now, as we lay pinned to the ground – she by her infirmity, me by her dead weight – I caught a fleeting glimpse of a look that I had never seen before, a look that might have been called haunted, if that were a less hackneyed term. But haunted really isn't strong enough, for there was something else going on that, even now, I can't quite find words for. I think that, when she fell again, the sick cow had understood, at some bone-deep level, that the old farmer wouldn't be able to save her, and my falling with her had probably confirmed her growing suspicion that these humans, these masters in whom she had placed so much trust, were nowhere near as omnipotent as she had been led to believe. We had, in fact, failed her – and as that knowledge hit home, she turned her head slightly and looked out through the entrance to the enclosure towards the nearby hedgerow, where something seemed to catch, and then hold her attention. Whatever that something was, it seemed to draw her in and, for a few seconds, she seemed illuminated, rapt. All of this happened in a matter of moments – and almost immediately, the old man somehow got me free and I struggled to my feet warily, half-expecting my legs to give way. The farmer looked at me and I saw for the first time that he had decided the cow was beyond saving and that he wanted me to know that I wasn't to blame. And I think, now, that I probably imagined it, but at the time, I thought that the old man was sad, not for the financial loss, but for the beast's sake. Or perhaps not sad, so much as sorry. Of course, he was too different from me for either of us to find some form of words, or even some tacit means of expression, that would have meant very much at all – and yet, for that one moment, I wanted to say something that might bring comfort to us both, whatever we were feeling. I wanted to make an effort at speech, even though I had been given to understand, implicitly, that in this neck of the woods, any form of articulacy was a sign of weakness, a character flaw that, where it existed at all, was confined to persons of dubious character. Maybe it was this knowledge that left me speechless, but I'll never know for sure, for at that moment the old farmer's son and another man appeared at the entrance to the small enclosure. The son looked at me, and then, at the fallen cow, his expression clearly implying that there had to be a connection between my obvious incompetence and her state of collapse. Then, working in complete silence, all four of us got the cow back on her feet and, though her heart was clearly not in it, and the old farmer had clearly decided that there was no hope of recovery, we went through the motions for what felt like a long time, only giving up when the animal's utter helplessness became too heavy to bear, at which point we went indoors so the old farmer could telephone the vet.

I have no wish to make more of this event than it merits. Such mishaps and consequent losses are routine on any farm and, whatever the humans in such stories may feel inwardly, they are obliged by custom and common sense to get on with the business of the day. A cow is a beast, a beast is livestock and livestock has a fixed commercial value. For me, however, things were slightly different. As an outsider, I could afford to indulge my feelings and think beyond the bounds of common sense, just as the old man and his even older son had always suspected I might – and I had no qualms at all about living up to their worst expectations. At the same time, some kind of obligation remains, an obligation not to indulge, not to make too much of this encounter. The moment I experienced in that yard was a moment of pity, no doubt, and I did not envy the dying cow her domesticated, and partly denatured existence. Yet I envied her something, nevertheless. For, whatever it was that she saw beyond that small enclosure where we lay stricken together, whatever she sensed just beyond our small circle of disappointment and defeat, she had seen something in its entirety that I had not, and she had felt it as a presence. Whereas I only got there by following her drifting attention. I have no good word for what I sensed, not just because I only sensed it vaguely, as through a glass darkly, but also because, in the vocabulary I have to hand, I cannot come up with a word to express what I felt. No word to express it for myself, and no word to communicate it to another. Whatever it was, it only lingered for the briefest of moments and, as much as I would have liked to turn just a little more and catch a fuller glimpse of the unsayable, it did not come good for me. It was, as I say, a small thing, a non-event, the merest impression that, even if I could not put my finger on it, I do not think I could explain it. But I felt the loss, nonetheless.

Over the last several years, plans to reintroduce wild aurochs across Europe, via a careful process of genetic engineering, have been advanced by such conservation bodies as The European Rewilding Network, with the hope that the establishment of viable wild populations will foster a regeneration of biodiversity-rich landscapes across the continent. This is a laudable aim, but it is by no means the first such project. In the 1930s, for example, Hermann Göring, an avid hunter who was always looking for new and more challenging quarry to pursue, invested heavily in an aurochs breeding program led by zoologist and S.S. member, Lutz Heck, who believed that, using Spanish fighting bulls and other breeds known for their aggressiveness, he could recreate the true wild aurochs through an ideologically driven process of selective breeding. The scheme excited Göring, who had long nurtured dreams of emulating Siegfried, the legendary hunter and giant killer of the anonymous thirteenth century epic poem, The *Nibelungenlied*, or *Song of the Nibelungs*, the prime source for Wagner's Ring Cycle libretti:

> Then an old huntsman took a good sleuth-hound and in a short space brought the lord to where many beasts were found. Whatso rose from its lair the comrades hunted as good hunters still are wont to do. Whatever the brach started, bold Siegfried, the hero of Netherland, slew with his hand. His horse did run so hard that none escaped him. In the chase he gained the prize above them all. Doughty enow he was in all things. The beast which he slew with his hands was the first, a mighty boar; after which he found full soon a monstrous lion. When the brach started this from its lair, he shot it with his bow, in which he had placed a full sharp arrow. After the shot the lion ran the space of but three bounds. The hunting fellowship gave Siegfried thanks. Thereafter he speedily slew a bison and an elk, four strong ure-oxen, and a savage shelk. Horse bare him so swiftly that naught escaped him, nor could hart or hind avoid him. Then the sleuth-hound found a mighty boar; when he began to flee, at once there came the master of the hunt and encountered him upon his path. Wrathfully the boar did run against the valiant hero, but Kriemhild's husband slew him with his sword.[16]

16 Anonymous: *The Nibelungenlied*, tr. by Daniel B. Shumway (1909) Houghton-Mifflin, New York.

After the National Socialists came to power, Göring, a self-professed animal lover and (unlike the Führer) an avid carnivore, appropriated state funds to create a fabulous hunting lodge at Schorfheide, around seventy kilometres north of Berlin. This he decorated with artworks by Botticelli, Dürer, Cranach, Velasquez and van Gogh, as well as tapestries, sculptures and Dutch Master drawings, all looted from private collections and museums across Europe. The lodge (in fact, a substantial country house, named Carinhall, after Göring's first wife) was designed by Werner March, architect of the Olympic Stadium where, at the 1936 Olympiad, Hitler's carefully choreographed demonstration of Aryan superiority was disrupted, not just by the achievements of Jesse Owens, Ralph Metcalfe, John Woodruff and several other African-American athletes, but also by a quirk of nature itself, recorded in an anecdotal account of the Games' opening ceremony by U.S. distance runner, Louis Zamperini:

> They released 25,000 pigeons, the sky was clouded with pigeons, the pigeons circled overhead, and then they shot a cannon, and they scared the poop out of the pigeons, and we had straw hats, flat straw hats, and you could hear the pitter-patter on our straw hats, but we felt sorry for the women, for they got it in their hair, but I mean there were a mass of droppings ...

No such embarrassment would be permitted to upset Göring's fantasies of Teutonic supremacy. Along with Heck and other insiders, he would re-enact scenes from German mythology, venturing with small hunting parties into Schorfheide Forest, sometimes clad in period costume and carrying only a spear, in pursuit of wild boar and other beasts, just as Siegfried had done. He did not get the aurochs he was hoping for, however. Though Lutz Heck would declare that 'the extinct aurochs has arisen again as a wild German species in the Third Reich', what he – and, in a separate suite of experiments, his brother Heinz – eventually produced was an animal that, while large and aggressive, was very different from the aurochs of old. After the war, much of the brothers' stock were labelled 'Nazi cattle' and destroyed, though a few survived, only to be soundly debunked by biological experts as no closer to the wild aurochs painted by the Altamira cave artists than many other breeds, with both Heck brothers characterised as complacent, slapdash in their approach, and more inclined to fantasy than to scientific rigour. In the end, Reichsjägermeister Göring and his friend Heck would never enjoy the dubious pleasure of hunting a true wild aurochs in the forests of Brandenburg, though history records that, in 1941, when Heck raided the Warsaw Zoo for prize specimens to enhance Berlin's Tierpark, he arranged for a private hunting party in the gardens, during which he and a group of fellow Nazis had a fine time slaughtering what was left of the Zoo's animal population. Once that cheery excursion was done with, the stricken venue was repurposed as a pig farm.

In the *Song of the Nibelungs*, Siegfried is murdered by his former hunting companion, Hagen and dies fighting, as a true hero must:

> When Lord Siegfried felt the mighty wound, up
> from the spring he started in a rage. From betwixt
> his shoulder blades a long spear-shaft towered. He
> weened to find his bow or his sword, and then had

> Hagen been repaid as he deserved. But when the sorely wounded hero found no trace of his sword, then had he naught else but his shield. This he snatched from the spring and ran at Hagen; nor could King Gunther's man escape him ... Had he had a sword in hand, then had it been Hagen's death, so sore enraged was the wounded man. Forsooth he had good cause thereof. His hue grew pale, he could not stand; his strength of body melted quite away, for in bright colours he bore the signs of death. Thereafter he was bewailed by fair dames enow.[17]

There were no fair dames for Göring and his tame eugenicist, however. When the Russians entered Berlin at the end of the war, Heck and his wife fled to Bavaria; he would go on to write a book about his travels in Africa and Canada and his work as director of the Berlin Zoo, published in English – 'with some omissions' [sic] – as *Animals: My Adventure*. As for Göring, history records that, having been sentenced to death at Nuremberg for a catalogue of war crimes, the man who had once been Hitler's designated successor evaded justice by swallowing potassium cyanide. The house at Carinhall, where he had hosted a tea party for Edward, Duke of Windsor and Wallis Simpson during their 1937 tour of Germany, was demolished on his orders not long before he was captured, leaving only ruins, over which Schorfheide Forest has re-established its hold. In recent years, the grounds have reverted to something resembling a nature park, with native trees and wild plants scrambling over what remains of the stonework. What had been Göring's bunker is now a bat reserve, while the land around the former estate has been absorbed into the Schorfheide-Chorin Biosphere

17 ibid

Reserve, where endangered animals like pond tortoises and fire-bellied toads, as well as cranes, black storks, ospreys and lesser spotted eagles find refuge in around 1300 square kilometres of pine woods, heath and re-natured bogs.

Yet while this project offers reasons for hope, it is also a signal of what has been lost. Maybe it is always so: there ought to be a science of nostalgia, which is often a far more complex, and more interesting phenomenon than we assume. Developers of all kinds work hard to defuse its power, either by appropriating it for political purposes (back-to-basics, warm beer and cricket on the village green, adherence to some mythical and thoroughly bowdlerised group of Founding Fathers or Ur-heroes) or by dismissing every act of resistance to their version of Progress as pure sentimentality. In fact, I am surely being sentimental now, when I imagine the aurochs wandering freely through Europe, just as they might have continued to do, had they survived us. Or rather, I imagine what kind of world this would be if they were still here, a world that would be more uncertain, no doubt, but all the more vital for that. A wilder world. A world less developed. Loss is inevitable, not only because human beings are careless and greedy, but because it is part of the natural cycle – and there is a fugitive, wistful beauty to be constructed from the absence of anything. Nothing ever vanishes, quite, without leaving behind some kind of trace, some vague shape or echo, even if it is only in the relicts of a culture: a ruin, a myth, a ritual whose true purpose is forgotten, but is still performed on the village green at Mayday and, so, can still infect young minds with pagan notions. That said, I continue to miss something I have never seen, and I would give a great deal to witness it, just once. No great event, just a summer's evening on a wide plain where, once upon a time, in Europe, a herd of aurochs has gathered for the night, the bulls standing sentinel in the moonlight, their faces attentive and calm as the wind ripples over the nearby lake and an elusive, inhuman music drifts from the darkening reeds.

The last aurochs died in Poland in the early seventeenth century. This noble species, larger and more powerful than the fighting bulls of Spain, had died out gradually from the south, its numbers falling until, by the mid-thirteenth century, the dwindling herds were confined to the wetlands and wilder landscapes of Eastern Europe and Prussia. In some areas, attempts at conservation were made, as the aurochs was considered a desirable quarry by those nobles and kings who, like Siegfried and his pals, reserved the right to hunt them (as always, wherever the great lord reigned, poaching was punishable by severe fines, torture, or even death). Over the next two centuries, changes in land use continued to encroach and, in spite of one final effort at conservation, the last known aurochs died on a game reserve in the Jaktorów Forest in 1627. Its horn was, of course, taken as a trophy and inscribed with the name of the lord of the estate where it had died (peacefully, of natural causes):

> Horn of the last aurochs from the Sochaczew Forest, from Stanisław Radziejowski, voivode of Rawa, at that time starost of Sochaczew.

Today, nothing remains of the true wild aurochs, other than those European 'rewilding' programmes – and a traditional music band called The Last Aurochs who describe themselves on their website as 'a gathering of trad musicians from different backgrounds based in the Inner West, Sydney,

Australia. We play modern arrangements of traditional tunes from known and lesser-known traditions such as Ireland, Scotland, France, Spain and Portugal, along with our own compositions and modern trad tunes.' The website entry adds that the group chose its name to honour 'the now extinct aurochs, the wild ancestor of domesticated cattle. The aurochs roamed most of Europe freely for centuries, until it was hunted to extinction. It represents the connections between different peoples as they hunted, worshiped, painted, and carved the aurochs for millennia.'

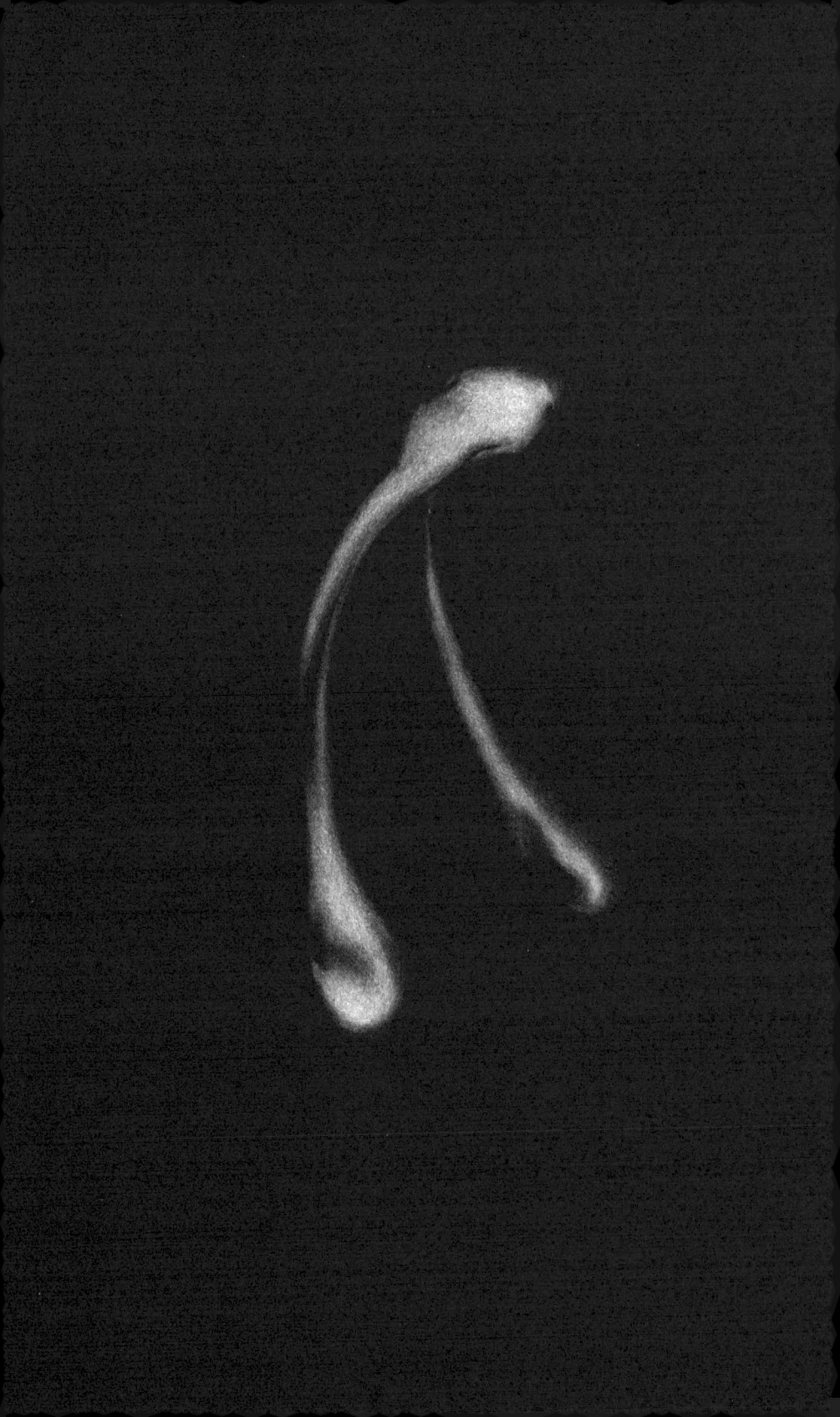

The hint half guessed, the gift half understood

I SOMETIMES WONDER if we know what we are saying, when we use the word *extinction*. The etymology is straightforward enough[18] and, unfortunately, we have had a good deal of practice in applying it, over the last fifty years in particular, but what does extinction mean *as a fact*? What happens when a bird or a tree-frog or an orchid vanishes forever? What is being expunged from the living record, and what are the ramifications and unexpected consequences of that loss?

What do all these extinctions – those we are aware of and because the pace of destruction is so rapid, those that flash by unnoticed – what does all this loss do, not only to the quality of the planetary *vie commune*, but also to the fabric of a collective human awareness?

That, perhaps, is the real question being raised by the much-maligned Extinction Rebellion (XR) movement, whose attempts to foster immediate and effective change have been met in England with what, effectively, amounts to state violence.

---

18 See the Online Etymological Dictionary:
Extinction: early 15c., 'annihilation,' from Latin extinctionem/exstinctionem (nominative extinctio/exstinctio) 'extinction, annihilation,' noun of action from past participle stem of extinguere/exstinguere 'quench, wipe out' (see *extinguish*). Originally of fires, lights; figurative use, the wiping out of a material thing (a debt, a person, a family, etc.) from early 17c.; of species by 1784.

Those involved in this group are a mix of seasoned activists and first-time protestors, people from all walks of life, from students to retirees, including 'doctors and delivery drivers, teachers and builders, even a retired merchant mariner in his 80s.' Their acts of civil disobedience have been overwhelmingly peaceful, yet police counter-terrorism units in the UK have been directed to treat them as dangerous extremists and the British Home Secretary, Priti Patel, has publicly characterised them as criminals, whose gatherings constitute 'a shameful attack on our way of life, our economy and the livelihoods of the hard-working majority.' The influential right-wing group, Policy Exchange (which describes itself as 'the UK's leading think tank…whose mission is to develop and promote new policy ideas that will deliver better public services, a stronger society and a more dynamic economy') has urged policy makers to crack down, claiming that:

> Extinction Rebellion is an extremist organisation whose methods need to be confronted and challenged rather than supported and condoned. If we fail to confront those who incite and encourage mass law-breaking, we fail in our duty to confront extremism. This new form of extremism needs to be tackled by Ministers and politicians, the Commission for Countering Extremism, police and the general public.[19]

For some reason, the Home Secretary employs very similar language when talking about XR. 'I refuse point blank to allow that kind of anarchy on our streets and I'm right behind you as you bring the full might of the law down upon that selfish minority,' she told a police conference in September 2020. 'The very criminals who disrupt our free society have

---

19 *Policy Exchange: Extremism Rebellion: A review of ideology and tactics* (2019). According to the transparency website, Transparify, Policy Exchange is one of only four think tanks in the UK who 'still consider it acceptable to take money from hidden hands behind closed doors.'

to be stopped and together we must all stand firm against the guerrilla tactics of Extinction Rebellion.' She went on to say that the police should 'adapt to the threat that they pose and ensure that justice is served ... Police have a whole range of powers at their disposal and they should be used ... against those who threaten our freedoms.'

It is hard, hearing these words, not to think of 1961, when the Commissioner of Public Safety [sic] for the city of Birmingham, Alabama, Eugene 'Bull' Connor proclaimed, with regard to the Civil Rights movement: 'As I have said on numerous occasions, we are not going to stand for [freedom riders] in Birmingham. And if necessary, we will fill the jail full and we don't care whose toes we step on. I am saying now to these meddlers from out of our city, the best thing for them to do is stay out if they don't want to get slapped in jail. Our people of Birmingham are a peaceful people and we never have any trouble here unless some people come into our city looking for trouble. And I've never seen anyone yet look for trouble who wasn't able to find it.'

As men like Bull Connor continued to dole out trouble across the South, John F. Kennedy was ultimately obliged to address the nation in the summer of 1963, just months before he was murdered. In a CBS broadcast from June 11 that year, he said: 'We face, therefore, a moral crisis as a country and as a people. It cannot be met by repressive police action. It cannot be left to increased demonstrations in the streets. It cannot be quieted by token moves or talk. It is time to act in the Congress, in your State and local legislative body and, above all, in all of our daily lives.'

> As Mark Twain is said to have observed: history may not repeat itself, but it sure does rhyme.

★

Extinction comes in many forms. When we talk about it, we tend to mention animals first, especially 'higher' mammals, but we acknowledge an associated threat to plants and insects, even if we do little to protect them. What we sometimes overlook is the fact that every loss matters. Nothing is inessential: the natural world is a fabric, not a ladder or a schematic tree. It makes no sense to draw one thread from that fabric and call it singularly important (or not) and worth saving (or not) for the fabric is, in essence, a continuum. In our public rhetoric, we like to talk about how 'interconnected' everything is, but this leads us to picture life as a network, or a lattice – that is, as an assemblage of connected, but distinct objects. At its crudest, this view conceives of 'Nature' as a great jigsaw puzzle in which each piece fits into its appointed place to make an overall picture, and the loss of any one piece leaves a visible but limited gap – but this is not how extinction works. The pieces of a jigsaw have edges, they are clearly defined and individual, the loss of one or two may be regrettable, but the picture remains more or less coherent. By contrast, there are no individual pieces in an ecology, everything is continuous with everything else, and the loss of one 'piece' impacts the whole in ways that we cannot predict, blurring the image, clouding the colours and lines. The loss of a piece in one area of the puzzle will have unforeseen consequences elsewhere, in a seemingly unrelated area of the picture, while many of the elements that maintain the whole are invisible to the viewer, hidden forces that are not located here or there or anywhere specific at all, but inform the totality in ways that, very often, we do not begin to understand until it is too late.

Not all extinctions can be attributed to human agency, of course – or not historically, at least. Because so many *have* happened since the start of the industrial revolution, we tend to assume that every species loss comes as a result of human dereliction, but some things slip away naturally, due to changing weather conditions, population shifts and other factors. In the interests of fairness, we can distinguish between what might be considered natural extinctions and those artificial or forced extinctions that result from human abuse (through overhunting, pollution, the impacts of runaway population growth or such human-engineered degradations of habitat as deforestation, desertification, paludification and ocean acidification)[20]. Nevertheless, it should surprise no-one to learn that the majority of recent extinctions have been caused by the sheer mass of humanity. There are now over seven-and-a-half billion of us and, across the globe, we are developing, harvesting and hunting wild creatures into oblivion, mostly through habitat destruction. At the same time, even as the recorded extinctions caused by this activity has set alarm bells ringing, they only reveal part of the problem. Many species are lost before we even know we are losing them, while official figures frequently lag behind the reality. Extinction researchers tend not to leap to judgement, and often do not publish their findings until they are very sure of their facts. Take, as just one example, the case of the Cunning Silverside, a Mexican freshwater fish that was last seen in 1957, but was only declared extinct in 2019 – lost for over sixty years, it remained in limbo until studies were finalised, at which point it officially disappeared. And the Cunning Silverside is by no means alone. All too often, extinction science resembles deep space research: what we see

---

20 In his introduction to the published version of 'The Great Auk, or Garefowl', a paper read by Thomas Parkin M. A. before the members of the Hastings and St. Leonards Natural History Society on June 28, 1894, W. C. J. Ruskin Butterfield says that we should see the loss of the Great Auk as a case of 'extermination rather than extinction', since 'extermination involves the idea of man's influence; while extinction is more applicable in those cases where a species has succumbed to the evolution of Natural Law.'

now actually happened long ago and, all too often, the dim light that we find in the darkness has already burned out. At the same time, each single extinction that we record can have subtle, non-immediate consequences, so that a black spot on the species map today may really represent a host of dark areas that our instruments have yet to register.

Forced extinction is the responsibility of humanity, as is the associated problem of extirpation, or local extinction, where a species dies out in one geographical location, but is not yet considered officially extinct, because other instances of that species exist elsewhere. It is all too easy to overlook the problems caused by this distinction but, to suggest a crude analogy, it would be foolish of me, say, to empty out my bank account and spend my entire savings on a golf club membership, or a ten year's supply of palm oil, in the mistaken belief that my cousin, who seems relatively affluent, will pay off my credit card debts and sub me for the utilities bill next month – especially if my cousin shares my fatal passion for golf and palm oil. Meanwhile, another, less publicised problem arises around the question of numbers. Many animal populations need to be plentiful in order to be truly viable, we cannot consider them safe unless they exist in huge shoals, large flocks, teeming swarms. When it comes to extinction, the measure of risk that needs to be applied is not just how many or how few individuals of a species remain, but how they live, and where, and how at home they are in their environment. In short, we need to assess the risks in terms of biomass (and gene pool diversity) as well as numbers.

At the same time, the identification of forced extinctions and extirpations should not be confined to animals and plants, or even to their habitats or flock sizes. Our concept of extinction should also include the devastating effects of development and enclosure on languages and regional dialects, philosophical or ritual traditions and cultural diversity. Also – though this may seem fanciful to some – we have to recognise the fact that time and space themselves are at risk. Finally (and this seems less fanciful with each passing day) our inner spaces are being placed in jeopardy, as the providers of social media colonise and denature what use to be called *the life of the mind* for advertising revenues or political gain. Science fiction not so long ago, the enclosure of experience itself – not only of our consumer tastes, but also of our root desires, our dreams, our political leanings – has become commonplace. From habitat to place itself, from public to inner space, from freedom of speech to the chambers of our imagery[21], everything is subject to enclosure, all too often by powers and principalities that we cannot even name.

Recent years have seen a massive expansion in the loss of place. Not just habitats, but sacred sites, burial grounds, city districts, ancient pathways and even horizons have vanished. Any sense of wilderness and no man's land that remains to us is in process of decay. Everything that can be appropriated has been enclosed, tamed, conditioned, redefined and reallocated as 'resources.' Quotidian life has become increasingly virtual – and is constantly under surveillance. As social media bots come to 'know' more about who we are than we do, what passes for the life of the mind is increasingly enclosed and denatured. Our dreams and our desires are engineered by

---

21 See Ezekiel 8:12: 'Then said he unto me, Son of man, hast thou seen what the ancients of the house of Israel do in the dark, every man in the chambers of his imagery?'

algorithms that persuade us, more or less subliminally, to buy ever more consumer junk that we neither want nor need (and, since it is all too often made from plastic and is subject to rapidly changing fashions, much of it ends up fouling the ocean). Similar algorithms persuade us to vote for the politicians who are least likely to champion the land against large corporations and energy interests. At the same time, self-esteem depends on a retweet, a like, or a tag. By now, even the metaphysical is being enclosed – so much so that even *nowhere*, that space beyond conscious deliberation from which ideas and inspiration can inexplicably appear, is close to extinct, as a character in Don DeLillo's 2020 novel, *The Silence*, points out:

> There is almost nothing left of nowhere. When a missing fact emerges without digital assistance, each person announces it to the other while looking off into a remote distance, the otherworld of what was known and lost.[22]

Nowhere is the source of unbidden memories, the hinterland where poetry and improvisation and even the solutions to mathematical theorems breed. Many of our best ideas come out of nowhere, where the usual orthodoxies do not hold sway. When nothing is left of nowhere, all that remains is whatever passes for worldly authority. Church Dogma. The Age of Reason. Technological Progress. The Stock Exchange. Social Media.

What is surprising about all this is, not so much that it is happening, as that we are taking it so calmly, at least in public. True, there are regular documentaries on Netflix about everything that is going on, but even as we take note of our predicament, we continue to chase the same old illusions, purchasing the same overpriced junk, and tolerating the

22 Don DeLillo, *The Silence*, Scribner, New York, 2020.

same predictable public deceptions as we have always done. Runaway growth continues. The economic health of entire societies is measured according to the market value of its richest members, who rarely pay taxes. As we slide blindly into the virtual, debating alternative facts and watching whatever glib entertainments we are offered, the fabric of everyday life unravels – but that slide is almost obscenely quiet. Writing in the 1840s, Søren Kierkegaard remarks that:

> The greatest hazard of all, losing one's self, can occur very quietly in the world, as if it were nothing at all. No other loss can occur so quietly; any other loss – an arm, a leg, five dollars, a wife, etc. – is sure to be noticed.[23]

Perhaps this is the last extinction that needs to be considered: a loss of humanity that stops short of physical extirpation to engineer the semi-witting abandonment of what Kierkegaard sees in selfhood as a 'synthesis in which the finite is the limiting factor, and the infinite the expanding factor.' Would it not be the ultimate irony if, after millennia of being here as thinking meat, we suffered such a quiet and docile loss of the inner life that, as we died away, none of us even noticed that the deluge was finally flooding in?

In public discourse, however, such metaphysical considerations barely come into play. As has been noted, our day-to-day concerns about extinction focus on the more likeable animals – pandas, say, or snow leopards: creatures that, for any number of reasons, we find 'relatable.' More recently, as catastrophic habitat loss has sporadically made

---

23 Søren Kierkegaard, *The Sickness Unto Death*, tr. Howard V. Hong and Edna H. Hong, Princeton University Press, 1983.

it to the nightly news, we have begun to worry, publicly, over a few iconic rainforests and, given the link with climate change, the Arctic icecaps. (Some outlets have even noted the possible link between habitat destruction and viral pandemics.) What we habitually overlook, however, is the threat to those creatures that we do not find relatable, just as we ignore intangible processes or forces that we cannot define as objects. In theory, we know that it is not enough to save or conserve individual species, or to set aside little islands of habitat as game parks or rewilding zones, but much of what we see in the media still focuses on such drives. This is not surprising. The media in general do not like complexity (it distracts from the advertising) and no matter how it is framed, extinction is a highly complex and multifaceted problem. It is also a 'downer'. Better a warm-hearted story about the apparent rescue of a single species or location. Better still, a global project in which photogenic children come together, under the sponsorship of a kindly corporation, to save an endangered tree frog. With such distractions at the feelgood tail-end of the nightly news, business can go on as usual: energy companies make a few cosmetic changes, hybrid cars continue to become more affordable and, all the while, new real estate gets developed and sold. Every day we lose overall diversity and wild biomass – and, every day, we lose a little more of what remains of *place*. Places we grew up in. Places that represented something of the wild. Meadows, shorelines, woods. Patches of no man's land between one executive housing estate and another. Like forests and wetlands, local places vanish and we barely notice; until, in the end, the nature of place itself comes into question. Aldo Leopold observes that:

> Much of the damage inflicted on land is quite
> invisible to laymen. An ecologist must either harden
> his shell and make believe that the consequences of

science are none of his business, or he must be the doctor who sees the marks of death in a community that believes itself well and does not want to be told otherwise.[24]

At the root of the loss of place is a fundamental confusion that is rarely acknowledged – and that confusion arises when we overlay place with what Leopold calls 'our Abrahamic concept of land.'[25] Because we accept the idea that land can be privately owned, we tacitly permit the ownership of place. Yet, while I may not need land to survive, I do need a place to live. Place and time are the ground of all being. We have to be somewhere (here) at a point in time (now) and what it means to *be here, now* depends on how we see, use and care for place – which is to say, who owns (and, so, who cares for or exploits) the world.

The absurdity of the notion that the land can be property was succinctly expressed by Jean-Jacques Rousseau in 1762: 'The first person who, having enclosed a plot of land, took it into his head to say this is mine and found people simple enough to believe him was the true founder of civil society. What crimes, wars, murders, what miseries and horrors would the human

---

24 Aldo Leopold: *A Sand County Almanac*, Oxford University Press, USA

25 See Genesis 1:28 – 30: 'And God blessed them, and God said unto them, Be fruitful, and multiply, and replenish the earth, and subdue it: and have dominion over the fish of the sea, and over the fowl of the air, and over every living thing that moveth upon the earth.

And God said, Behold, I have given you every herb bearing seed, which is upon the face of all the earth, and every tree, in the which is the fruit of a tree yielding seed; to you it shall be for meat.

And to every beast of the earth, and to every fowl of the air, and to every thing that creepeth upon the earth, wherein there is life, I have given every green herb for meat: and it was so.'

race have been spared, had someone pulled up the stakes or filled in the ditch and cried out to his fellow men: 'Do not listen to this imposter. You are lost if you forget that the fruits of the earth belong to all and the earth to no one!"

These lines (from *On the Social Contract; or, Principles of Political Rights*) form the epigraph to Marion Shoard's *This Land Is Our Land*, in which the author explores, not only the damage inflicted on the land by an Abrahamic system of ownership, but also the degradation of day-to-day experience that comes of an underlying sense of displacement[26]:

> As the third Millennium approaches, land is coming to be seen once more as a key human resource and therefore a prime focus of conflict. During a century dominated by urbanization and industrialization, it has often seemed as if the earth itself were an issue we could relegate to the past. We seemed able to concern ourselves exclusively with technologies of satisfaction which have broken free of the ancient preoccupation with the soil to which humanity's activities and aspirations seemed irrevocably tied for so long. But no longer. With the shock of a sleeper rising from a diverting dream, we are being forced to the realization that we can have no virtual existence without corporeal reality, that our corporeal selves cannot exist without a satisfactory relationship with our physical surroundings. It grows ever more apparent that to survive and fulfil ourselves we are going to have to struggle to impose our will on those surroundings in ways in which our ancestors could not have imagined.

If we follow this argument to its conclusion, we can see that the loss of our land, often to remote, anonymous owners and management companies who see it purely as an exploitable

---

26 Marion Shoard, *This Land is Our Land*, Paladin, 1987.

resource, leads to a loss of the meaningful presence that place offers. As Shoard writes in her Epilogue:

> For the first thousand years after the birth of Christ the land of Britain was effectively in the hands of its people. The last thousand years have been a kind of dark age in which the people have been shunted into a landless wilderness while the few have lorded it over their space.[27]

Shoard goes on to advocate for a reclamation of land and place – a reclamation devoutly to be wished. That it has failed to happen in the two dozen years since *This Land Is Our Land* was first published is one cause for regret, but the fact is that, in those intervening years, further enclosures of land, habitat, public space and even the life of the mind has displaced us even further from a world that should have been increasingly open to the invention of home.

That home is not a given, that it must be invented, is a fact of life for a species that, unlike foxes and the birds of the air, has no place to lay its head. Home is predicated on dwelling, and dwelling is predicated on place. But what is place? How do we know where one place ends and another begins? Do we find place, or do we make it? Perhaps both: we find a place, we give it a name, and we begin to change its intrinsic nature – and, sometimes, if we are unlucky enough to fall into the trap of Rousseau's imposter, we allow it to be transformed into property. Some pioneering type plants a flag. A legal type draws up deeds. The imposter says, 'This is mine', and nobody considers the absurdity of such a position. If we are

27 ibid

unlucky or foolish enough, we not only take the imposter at his word, but go to work to enclose more land, develop more resources and, in time, fill his coffers to overflowing. In the evolution of an Abrahamic society, the main reason for altering the lay of the land is to facilitate this process of galloping acquisition. This means that, all too often, our first relationship to place is a betrayal. Land ownership inevitably leads, first, to the denaturing of place and, second, to the basic conditions for social injustice. If one person or group has the right to enclose, develop or colonise an area, then others are not only excluded from its use, but also coerced into a position where their relationship to the land quickly becomes distorted. As the land around his home ground of Helpston was enclosed in the 1810s and 1820s, John Clare gave poignant voice to the end of a natural belonging in his poem, 'The Mores':

> These paths are stopt – the rude philistine's thrall
> Is laid upon them and destroyed them all
> Each little tyrant with his little sign
> Shows where man claims earth glows no more divine
> But paths to freedom and to childhood dear
> A board sticks up to notice 'no road here'
> And on the tree with ivy overhung
> The hated sign by vulgar taste is hung
> As tho' the very birds should learn to know
> When they go there they must no further go
> Thus, with the poor, scared freedom bade goodbye
> And much they feel it in the smothered sigh
> And birds and trees and flowers without a name
> All sighed when lawless law's enclosure came

Much has been made of Clare's insanity – but is it so very surprising that, uprooted from all that he knew and forced to witness the destruction of all that he loved, a sensitive man might be driven to madness – or, perhaps, to that other form of distraction, grief, which has lain buried in each of us since the first imposter claimed the first tract of land to do with as he pleased?

The extent to which we inhabit a place defines our relationship to the world as a whole – or to adopt Martin Heidegger's categories: to mortals (i.e. other living things), to the earth and the sky, and to the divinities (not gods in the conventional sense, but anonymous, informing or presiding spirits in the land: presences that, even if they are glimpsed in a given form, like Grahame's Dawn Piper, are not defined by, or confined to, any fixed condition). Where we allow a place to follow its given nature, living alongside other creatures in a biotic *vie commune* – where we *save* the world, so to speak – this is right dwelling. If we study the nature of a place in order to make ourselves at home there with a minimum of intervention, this is sustainable living. As we have learned from history, everything else is damage, blurring the fine boundaries between one place and another, denaturing what we have been given to share so that it can be reconstituted as property. Once land – once *place* – becomes property, it is no longer holy; that is, it is no longer, as the oldest etymology of the word 'holy' suggests, something 'that must be preserved whole or intact, that cannot be transgressed or violated.' When the world is parcelled out as tracts of land that may be owned, enclosed and exchanged for money, then the world is no longer whole. It is broken up. It becomes organically discontinuous. Because it is forever vulnerable to the whims of its owner, land that belongs to someone is no longer land where anyone can meaningfully belong.

★

The sense of place as something other than property is anathema to the developer. What the developer wants is not a holy place, but 'empty' *spaces*, areas of no man's land and dead zones that can be depicted as derelict or featureless, with no intrinsic value, and no history. The presence of certain species can undermine this depiction – which is why, in the countryside, it is common practice for developers and landowners to poison rare birds, or 'accidentally' spray old meadowlands with hardcore herbicides, before applying for planning permission on sensitive sites. One plot of land acquired for development used to have a badger sett; at another, peregrine falcons used to nest in the nearby quarry. Planning regulations are supposed to protect these things, but planning regulations are interpreted and applied by local politicians with contacts, campaign chests and long-standing obligations to vested interests. Even if local people or public pressure slows or temporarily halts a 'development', planning laws are written in such a way that developers can either appeal (there is little recourse for objectors once a development is approved) or renew their attack by reframing an application and starting again. Given the resources available to landowners and corporations, the quest for approval becomes a simple waiting game. Political pressure is brought to bear, PR campaigns are ramped up, bribes, in the form of 'community benefits' may be offered to key local 'stakeholders'. All of this busy-ness is aimed at perpetuating a kind of amnesia, a *forgetting* that what we mean by place is not a location, but the *nature* of that location: its history, its atmosphere, its ecology. Strip these things away, or damage them effectively enough, and place can be redesignated as space. Empty. Desolate. A waste land, ripe for improvement.

In reality, however, this empty space beloved of developers does not exist. Places can be degraded but, as long as they are not subjected to constant, unrelenting development, they can recover – as long as there are still *ruins* of some kind. Unlike development, which renders place nondescript, or generic, ruins are signs of continuity. Ruins are healthy. Seeds blow or wash into the footings of fallen houses, honeysuckle and Old Man's Beard scramble over fallen rubble, bees drift in to feed on the new blossom, birds nest in what remains of an old smokestack. All ruins are precious, and the costlier the ruination is, the more important it is to leave those ruins to stand. In his 1804 play, *Wilhelm Tell*, Schiller has the line: *neues Leben blüht aus den Ruinen: New life blooms from the ruins.* That new life is precious for its own sake, but it also forms a connection to the past, a visible sign of continuity. Of the natural cycle. *Where there is ruin*, says Rumi, *there is hope for a treasure.* The nature of that treasure may be difficult to decipher at first – but the fact remains that all ruins contain the promise of regeneration.

Take Chernobyl-Pripyat, for example. Twenty-five years after the nuclear accident there, back in April 1986, when the power plant's No. 4 reactor exploded, studies began to suggest that the expected ecological disaster had not, in fact, come about. Indeed, for the wildlife around Chernobyl, things could scarcely have been better. In 2011, when biological researchers from Texas Tech travelled to the area, they were taken aback to find a kind of modern-day Shangri-La that, in spite of the high radiation count, was lush, diverse and swarming with animal, bird and insect life. Admittedly, this had come about due to a happy accident, as Ron Chesser, a radiation biologist with the team, pointed out: 'proximity to the reactor has very little to do with how much radiation dose an organism is experiencing. You can come to the reactor from the east and actually not experience a huge change in the radiation background. However, if you approach it from the west . . . you'll see a very dramatic increase ....' In other words, while there was no denying that high levels of radiation were detectable, the prevailing wind conditions at the time of the accident meant that the toxicity was unevenly spread and drifted mostly westward, creating a new less exposed – and because humans had abandoned it, a newly safe – exclusion zone for wildlife to the east. Even with that qualification, however, the natural abundance that the researchers found in the safe zone was astonishing. In fact, given the evidence, the director of Texas Tech's Natural Science Research Laboratory, Robert Baker, found himself characterising that 20-mile exclusion zone in Edenic terms, 'The countryside is beautiful,' he said. 'The animals and plants are in greater numbers now than if the reactor had not gone down. The ecosystem is as it was before humans started living out there – except for the radiation.' And he continued: 'It seems as though normal human activities associated with agrarian society are more destructive than the world's worst nuclear meltdown.'

In short, given the choice between continuous human occupation and nuclear disaster followed by the absence of humans, the natural environment fared better with the latter – and, not surprisingly, Baker's remarks set environmentalists thinking. Might it be that, to save the planet's ecosystems from ourselves, we needed not one, but many Chernobyls?

Well, not as such; though some observers suspect that this is what some powerful players have begun to envisage – though their motives may have more to do with personal power than ecology. 'It may be quite possible that the global elite may be willing to allow current nuclear plants to continue to deteriorate and become hazardous because they provide the means by which conservation lands could be established,' says Susanne Posel, the chief editor of Occupy Corporatism. 'By using their globalist think-tank universities and controlled arsenal of scientists, the radioactive effects could be amplified in the public's perception, simply as a ruse to keep humans off the land. If this scheme were successful, eventually there could be massive areas of land deemed uninhabitable for humans across the globe, simply by allowing a nuclear disaster to occur.' The point here is that the rich might use disasters like Chernobyl to create no-go areas around safe havens for their own, very exclusive communities, which sounds like an extreme, conspiracy-theory perspective, but the question must be asked: Is there anything that we might realistically consider as beyond the moral limits of the global power elite? We are not talking about lizard-people stalking the corridors of Davos here, or secret cabals of deep state operatives; this is a valid question to ask of a billionaire class who control governments and institutions across the world via political donations, lobbying and plain old-fashioned corruption. If the planet is about to turn inhospitable, can enough of it be saved to accommodate their secret bunkers, private islands and high-security hilltop retreats while they wait out the storm? If ever there was a case of property values over holiness, that would be it.

Yet as cynical as this scenario may sound, it is hard, in the current climate, to dismiss it out of hand. If it has taught us nothing else, the Covid-19 pandemic has shown how casually those in power disregard any and all threats to the ninety-nine percent.

On the other hand, there is much that Chernobyl can teach us – and its first lesson might be that we need to allow ruin to come, when it is timely, rather than (re-)developing everything into extinction. Or, as Robinson Jeffers suggests in the 1938 poem 'Carmel Point', we must learn to

> unhumanize our views a little, and become confident
> As the rock and ocean that we were made from.

Against all expectations, the ruins of Chernobyl are beautiful. It was, at first, a terrible kind of beauty, and the human costs were intolerable but, now that it is there, we owe it to the people of the region to learn from it. Chernobyl is beautiful, the ruined city of Pripyat is beautiful – and anyone compiling a list of the postmodern wonders of the world would have to give these sites the most serious consideration. But there is more to it than that. Chernobyl-Pripyat is a true ruin – and ruins are always precious. Without ruins, we are condemned to grieve endlessly, with no possibility of healing; without ruins, we are doomed to an interminable round of developing and cleaning up and redeveloping, over and over again to no real end. Development declares itself good for utilitarian reasons – it is new, it is tidy, it provides amenities that are considered beneficial by any reasonable citizen – but it overlooks those aspects of place that cannot be quantified or turned for a profit. It comes as no surprise to hear developers talking about tradition, heritage and that catch-all phrase 'a sense of place.' But as J. B. Jackson points out, it is a phrase that means very little today:

> It is an awkward and ambiguous modern translation of the Latin term *genius loci*. In classical times it meant not so much the place itself as the guardian divinity of that place. It was believed that a locality – a space or a structure or a whole community – derived much of its unique quality from the presence or guardianship of a supernatural spirit. The visitor and the inhabitants were always aware of that benign presence and paid reverence to it on many occasions. The phrase thus implied celebration or ritual, and the location itself acquired a special status. Our

modern culture rejected the notion of a divine or supernatural presence, and in the eighteenth century the Latin phrase was usually translated as 'the genius of a place', meaning its influence.[28]

In the spirit of that modern culture, it no doubt seems fanciful to suggest that, at a basic, private, partly subliminal level, we still feel a sense of loss for the true *genius loci*, as well as a suspension of the celebrations and rituals associated with holy places. That loss gives rise to a hidden suspicion of lack, and so to a grief that we cannot expiate or even express. Publicly, we cannot name this grief and have it taken seriously – and if anyone were to suggest that it had to do with the loss of some old god, some *genius loci*, or with any kind of extinction, their arguments would be dismissed as sentimental. There are no official ceremonies to mourn such losses, there is no ritual to mark the passing of place. Instead, we cradle lack in our hearts and, when the opportunity arises, we let it out, just a little, on whatever pretext makes itself available, directing it at something more socially acceptable than the raw, guilty horror of having lost our place in the world. Our grief for place expresses itself by proxy, usually through a public event like the death of a pop star, or a highly-publicised catastrophe. A crashed airliner; a wrecked train. Or, for some English folk, a royal funeral.

When Princess Diana died, on 31 August 1997, a spontaneous outpouring of public grief was unloosed. As this period of unexpected mourning began, I was visiting friends in Orkney, so I started the week reasonably far from, and mostly

---

28 J. B. Jackson: 'A Sense of Place, a Sense of Time', *Design Quarterly*, no. 164, 1995.

unaware of, the grieving crowds. The sad events of that Paris night did, of course, register in Stromness and Kirkwall but, overall, the public response there was more respectful than excessive. Six days on, however, when I flew into Glasgow, I found George Square literally carpeted with floral tributes and, as I continued my homeward journey to Fife, I was struck by an almost palpable, near-universal air of mourning. Two days later, on a rambling trip through England that ended in London, it became clear that, the denser the area of population in which I found myself, the more urgent, and the more puzzling, that grief became. By that time, of course, the most narcissistic echelons of the celebrity class and, of course, the mainstream media, had rushed in to capitalise on the public mood, a mood at once powerful and lacking in focus, but even if these factors had not been in play, the grief expressed throughout that massive, utterly sincere display of communal, but not official, mourning could not be denied – even if, at times, it seemed decidedly performative.

At the same time, that grief was becoming rather muddled and inchoate – and I, like many others, began to doubt that it was all about this woman who, as decent and kind as she surely was, did not seem sufficiently commanding a figure to invoke such strong feelings amongst so many. Nevertheless, there was no doubting the fact that most of the grief was genuine and, though nobody asked, then, and few ask now what its true roots might be, I was convinced that it had deep and authentic roots in *something*. A real loss, pertinent to all; a national tragedy for which the death of an 'English Rose' became symbolic and, at some private level, synchronous with the loss of something more fundamental – something that, worn down by twenty years of a dog-eat-dog amorality, was finally beginning to crumble, like our sea-coasts, or the tilth of our over-farmed soil. A loss, not of one English Rose, but of England itself.

By then, a certain awareness of avoidable loss had dwelt in England for many decades, marked in passing by poets like John Clare, or T.S. Eliot, and gradually becoming less specific, and more existential: a matter, to paraphrase Philip Larkin, not only of guildhalls and carved choirs, but also of the very fabric of the land itself. Shadows. Meadows. The lanes. Today, this sense of 'England gone' is matched everywhere: we feel ourselves losing, not only the most valued ecosystems, (the decaying Arctic; the burning rainforests) that Climate Change permits us to mourn, but also a random and seemingly personal geography of local spaces that nobody else cares about. The copse where we played as children. A patch of undeveloped land, spotted with wildflowers, that we used to pass on the way to work. A row of allotments or a little park between city blocks, clawed back from public enjoyment and enclosed for yet another nondescript 'development.' At times, we cannot even point to anything specific; there is just a vague sense of enclosure. A loss of privacy, or continuity, or plain old mystery. There is no way to voice this sense of loss – and so it lingers, unspoken:

> People tend to suppress that which they cannot express. If an experience resists ready communication, a common response... is to deem it private – even idiosyncratic – and hence unimportant. In the large literature on environmental quality, relatively few works attempt to understand how people feel about space and place...[29]

Too vague or unimportant to be given a forum or any kind of ceremonial outlet, these local griefs are contained, hidden, suppressed – until some greater public event, often far removed from the original loss, creates a space, a theatre, as it were,

---

29 Yi-Fu Tuan, *Space and Place: the Perspective of Experience*, University of Minnesota Press, 1977.

for the communal performance of private mourning. So it is that, quietly, in murmurs, we grieve for the fabric of our lives – more, perhaps, than we grieve for the listed buildings and monuments – but that grief is too nebulous to be brought into the light of *la vie commune*. It is more permissible to grieve for a dead celebrity than for England, or even for the earth itself, which means that our sorrow is denied its full seriousness. We know, of course, why the crowd that gathers to mark a royal funeral is worthy of our pity, while the XR crowd that assembles to mourn our lost places and the creatures who once lived there must be criminalised – for we know that the politically powerful cannot admit that ecocide is happening. This knowledge, however, only deepens our dismay: apparently powerless to stop the destruction that we are witnessing, we are obliged to grieve, not just for the earth, but also for ourselves – that is, for a people denatured. A people that has become greedy, anxious, less spontaneous and, at the same time, disastrously more susceptible to the whims of its technology. This grief is all the more painful because it is shot through with a guilt from which no one is exempt. For, according to the accepted environmental / Climate Change narrative, we are obliged to accept that everyone is equally guilty, even though it always seems to be one small and shamelessly entitled group that profits most from the destruction.

Everyone, each and every grown-up child, has their own lost world. To speak of that world, however, is a risk: to recollect lost places is to reveal oneself as a victim of nostalgia, a condition diagnosed, literally, as a social disease in the nineteenth century. To remember that, once, there were more birds and butterflies in the woods, to notice that the patch of semi-wilderness behind the old sorting office is now a car park, is to confess to the most pitiful of sins: mere sentimentality. Yet something is gone, and to pretend that loss is neither here nor there is the real sin – for, whatever anybody says, the anonymous corporate and municipal dead-zones that stand here now are beyond forgiveness. They are beyond forgiveness, not just because they degrade the land, as such, but also because they steal our best places and moments. Childhood escapes. Romantic assignations. Moments of solitude and quiet in the midst of the day. That stand of holly or yew at the end of the lane, right next to the old postbox, where the snow always seemed to begin, new flakes drifting through the branches as you walked home from school or the office.

When I think of England gone, I think of a garden in the West Midlands, a place I once found by purest chance. I came upon it in the middle of a long, hot summer, many years ago. A friend and I parked her car at the end of a deep lane, where the woods opened out to grass and limestone, the only buildings immediately visible a few houses and a recently abandoned Post Office, its windows powdered with soot and dust. Directly opposite, but set back a few metres from the road, the shipwreck of a church stood – is it only the English who know that whatever deity still subsists in our time, it only takes up residency when the church is disused or empty? – and a few metres further still, just off to one side along a narrow gravel path, there was a garden.

Needless to say, my friend and I spent the afternoon there, and it was one of the happiest afternoons I can recall; but I will not describe the place further, or give directions, or name it, because it is gone now and I want to keep its secrets. I can go there in my mind's eye, but when I do, I must prepare myself for a grief that, as much as it acknowledges other, associated losses (of my companion on that day, for example, and unsurprisingly, of the younger man that I was then) it cannot be divorced from the memory of that place. And that grief is private, which means that it cannot be expressed as part of *la vie commune*. As Susan Stewart writes[30]:

> elegists have discovered that lyric sequences can provide a powerful means of addressing the tensions between grief's inchoate emotion and social rituals of mourning … How deeply we might comprehend formal expressions of grief, and whether such comprehension leads to understanding and sympathy, remain open questions. Recent prose memoirs … trace a mourner's growing self-knowledge as her life is changed and the dead come into clearer, often disconcerting, perspective. These narrative accounts of traumatic loss necessarily repeat and encompass it, acknowledging, if not an afterlife, at least an aftermath.

The outcome of this process may be, not just a personal resolution of grief, but the public, or semi-public performance of what Stewart calls 'the tension – famously explained by Freud – between melancholia, an endless process of painful repetition, and mourning, with its gradual movement toward closure.' It is this distinction – between melancholia and mourning – that must be recovered, for the sake of all who grieve, not for some golden age that never was, but for a land that was once visibly richer and more diverse than it is now. For it is through such a distinction that our individual experiences of grief for personal losses of place can be united with the individual griefs of others, transforming instances of melancholia – a condition that tends merely to repeat itself – into convivial rites of mourning that, by their very nature, offer shared experiences of closure and, if well conducted, active healing.

★

30 Susan Stewart: 'Discandied: On Women and Elegy', in *The Nation*, August 24, 2011.

It may be that I am reading too much into all of this. Perhaps our griefs really are smaller and more personal than I imagine. Yet I am not alone in suspecting that many of us feel burdened and borne down by a near-unbearable nostalgia, not only for lost places, but also for the other animals. Or not just for these, but for a wildness in which to seek and find our place alongside the creatures we have not yet rendered extinct, whether it be as totem builders moving through a continuum of glances, territorial negotiations and occasional affinities, or by imagining ourselves provisionally and temporarily at home on the great chain of being, somewhere – Heaven help us – between the beasts of the field and the seraphim. There is no question that we must desist from eliminating other species and their habitats for *their* sake (that remains as a moral challenge, and a point of honour) but the work of 'saving' the biosphere is work that we are obliged to do for other reasons – reasons that are difficult to put into words and, for some, may well be close to subliminal. Paul Shepard says it well in an essay titled 'What Good Are Animals':

> We will save them, if at all, because without them we are lost. Though lost we may survive, but what we will then be cannot be foreseen. We will imagine we are all things and fear all things. The distance between us and the jellyfish and earthworms will increase, alienating us farther from the Earth. A 'silent spring' will be nothing compared to the green prison of nature. The means of thinking through the difficult understanding of our humanity will be gone. We will be lost because wild mammals and birds are a magic monkey paw, a wishbone, a rabbit's foot that can enable us to love our own kind.

Those words were written in the late 1970s; how much more poignant they seem now will depend greatly on how thoroughly incorporated we have become into the virtual, enclosed, privatised world that has been created to contain us – by corporate fiat, to be sure, though it would be foolish to pretend that, as good consumers, we have not collaborated in the illusion. At the same time, it would be just as foolish to pretend that, for all but a handful of active dissenters, the sneaking suspicion that we are now as lost as Shepard suggests is a central concern for the entire 'developed' world. At the forefront of our minds, we care about our jobs and our families, we are anxious about galloping authoritarianism and the flagrant betrayals of fellow voters who have completely lost the plot. In fact, many of us *try not to think about it* – *it* being the very problem that Shepard calls 'the difficult understanding of our humanity.' Nevertheless, the grief remains. Somewhere at the back of the mind, it lingers. Wasn't there something we were charged with keeping? Were we not called upon to leave some space for other lives, other ways of being or, simply, places that, spared the awful burden of constant development, could go their own way, through the various forms of growth and ruin and decay characteristic of all things? Why is it that we have to 'develop' everywhere we go? Why is it that, every time we find a patch of wild land, or a great oak tree, or a swift-running river, we have to make our mark with a drainage project, or a carved heart, or a dam? The more lost we have become, the more we 'imagine we are all things and fear all things', the more we are compelled to impose ourselves on the world – that is, to *develop*. This is the disease of our time: we cannot leave anything alone. We do not use, we squander. We waste. We create wreckage and detritus. Ruin, decay, death – these are natural events and, left to occur naturally, they are beautiful to behold. Death leads to decay and decay feeds new life, renewal is cyclical, but it only happens when the circle is not broken. Schiller was right – *new life blooms from the ruins* – and this is always so. As every beginning biology student knows, it is a natural fact that all life blossoms amidst ruin of one kind or another, whether it be the proverbial corpse pushing up daisies or the steady rise of new life around Chernobyl. Ruin is the source of life, as long as we don't cover up every fallen city and patch of so-called waste land with new development schemes. And this is another of the paradoxes of our time: we grieve for the very things that we ourselves destroy, yes, and we grieve for the elusive, often unsayable lapses of attention and awareness that are the inevitable consequence of our distance from animal life, but we also mourn the spaces we destroy, the seeming absences that we fill for no good reason, the nowheres and the *terrae incognitae* that, once upon a time, allowed us, on the one hand, to dream of places that no human had ever seen before and, on the other, to know a little better where, and how precious home was.

There comes a time, somewhere in the midst, or perhaps towards the end of mourning, when we are able to say that, even though I still grieve for what is lost, I can affirm the beauty and the justness of everything that is loved, everything that is celebrated, everything that comes and goes in this world, not just for its own sake, but for the fact of love itself, the fact of celebration, the fact of transience. The fact of being. Sometimes this happens accidentally, or by proxy: the official ceremony is meant to mark something else entirely, but it leaves space for the unofficial to slip through.

On January 19, 2021, for instance, as they prepared to assume power, and so to take responsibility for the mess left to them, not only by Donald Trump but the entire Republican apparatus, Joe Biden and Kamala Harris visited the Lincoln Monument's iconic Reflecting Pool in Washington D.C. to pay their respects to the four hundred thousand Americans who had died in the Covid-19 pandemic up to that point. As they arrived, the scene was muted, the air a soft, dusty grey in the city twilight – and the sense of crepuscule continued while Cardinal Wilton Gregory, Archbishop of Washington, offered up prayers for the dead, followed by Vice-President Elect Harris, who suggested that, while 'for many months we have grieved by ourselves', the time had come 'to emerge from this ordeal with a new wisdom, to cherish simple moments, to imagine new possibilities and to open our hearts, just a little bit more, to one another.' As she spoke, it seemed probable that, unless America's ingrained racism blocked the way, I was listening to the next-but-one president of the United States, and it was hard not to wonder what her real position was on the environmental issues that faced Americans that night. Officially, she supported the Green New Deal: 'Climate change is an existential threat, and confronting it requires bold action. I'm a proud co-sponsor of Senator Markey's Green New Deal resolution,' she had said, in the spring of 2019. 'Political stunts won't get us anywhere. Combatting this crisis first requires the Republican majority to stop denying science and finally admit that climate change is real, and humans are the dominant cause. Then we can get serious about taking action to tackle the climate crisis at the scale of the problem.' But how much of that was political rhetoric? And how much would even the most environmentally committed politician be able to achieve, while mopping up the mess left by the previous administration, in the face of a governmental system visibly corrupted by commercial interests? It was clear, from the attack on the Capitol two weeks earlier, that Trumpism was alive and well and waiting for its next moment. What hope was there, really, that the political class, their campaigns funded by polluters and developers, would rush in where previous angels had feared to tread?

Next, after Harris had finished speaking, Lori Marie Key, a

twenty-nine-year-old nurse from Belleville, Michigan, stepped up to sing – what else but 'Amazing Grace'? Then Joe Biden approached the microphone. Quietly, with a self-restraint that seemed likeably out-of-place after four years of Trump, he spoke simply and, to all appearances, from the heart. 'To heal, we must remember,' he said, 'and it's hard, sometimes, to remember. But that's how we heal ... Between sundown and dusk, let us shine the lights in the darkness along the sacred pool of reflection and remember all who we lost.' As he spoke these words, an installation of four hundred columns, one for each thousand dead, lit up in a long, sweeping flow of liquid gold, all the way to the farthest edge of the pool, and as if to the Washington Monument beyond. With no crowds, and not much fanfare, this scene was, for a brief moment, rather moving – and though that brief moment ended abruptly with an *almost* forgivably out-of-context performance of Leonard Cohen's 'Hallelujah', it resumed for another, longer moment as soon as the song ended and the handful of people there present stood, bowed and silent, with no other sound but the faraway hum of traffic, the sky clear over their heads, the warm columns of gold light reflecting in the still grey water of the pool. It had been a ceremony to mourn four hundred thousand specific American dead, but it was not difficult to see it as something more general, a rite that, were it stripped of its cultural and religious overtones, might speak simply and honestly of all that had been lost until that moment, and all that would continue to be lost. One day, to mark a turning point that is the only alternative to annihilation, a similar ceremony may be enacted for all the species, places, spaces, dialects and indigenous peoples that we have squandered. A light in the pool for the aurochs and the auk, amongst all the others, a light lit by a humanity that had finally grown into its best role in the play of life, a role that Heidegger calls 'the shepherd of Being.' That would be something to see.

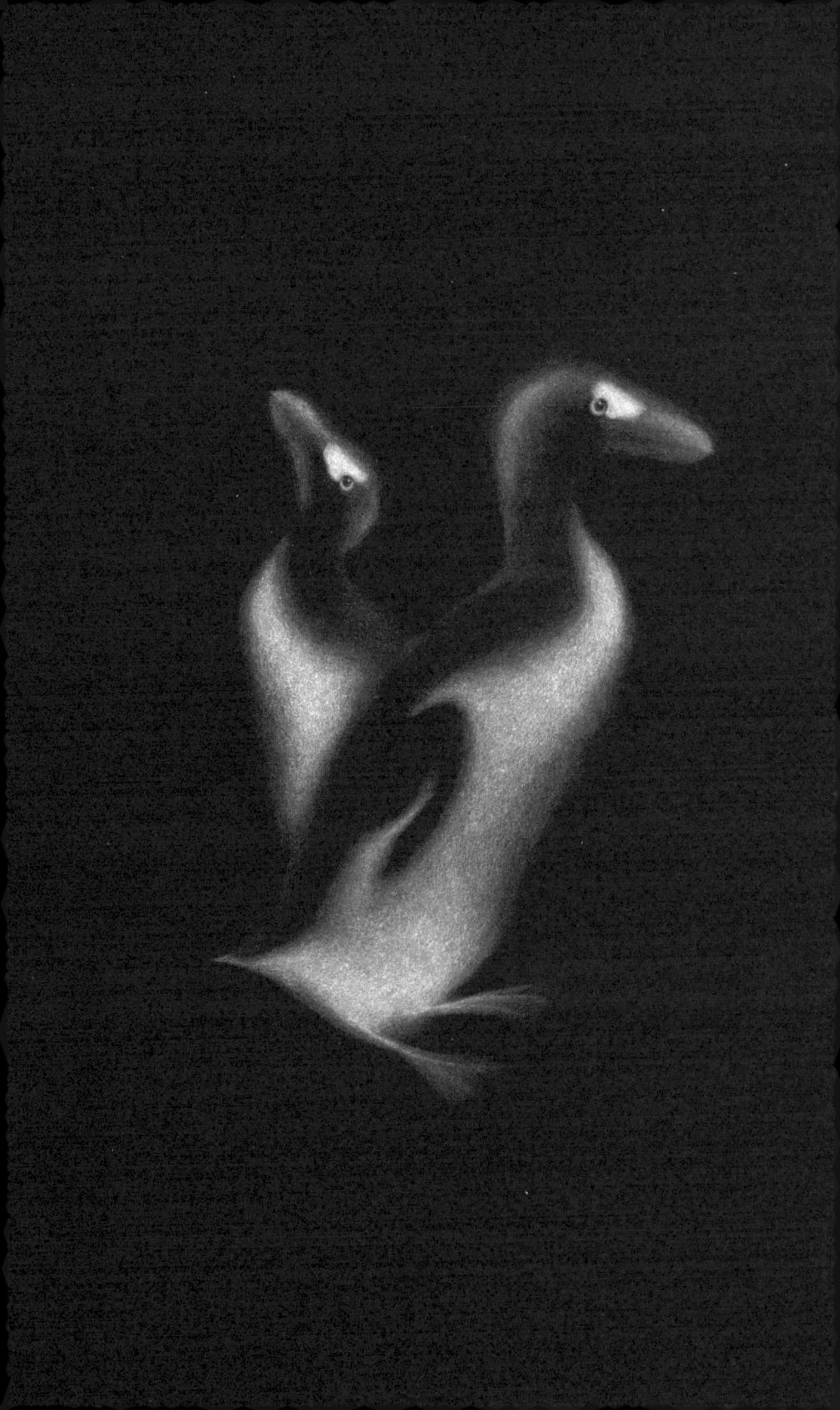

Auks

ONCE UPON A TIME, there were three men. In a traditional once-upon-a-time story, these men would be brothers – but, just for today, they are not. They *are* from Iceland, however, which is the next best thing: according to local legend, all Icelanders are descended from the country's national hero, Jón Arason, a Catholic bishop and poet who was beheaded in 1550, along with two of his sons, for leading a rebellion against the Danish overlord, King Christian III. This limited genealogy might seem hard to credit, but even if it is not strictly true, we do know that the people of Iceland can at least trace their origins to a small group of Viking colonists who settled there sometime in the late ninth century. So whatever the history, this narrative could be about three kinsmen from the north who, as is the custom in such tales, are given a quest to pursue, for which there will be a specified reward. Traditionally, such a narrative would tell how the first brother fails to win through, as does the second, leaving the youngest to step up and try his hand. Nobody expects him to succeed, given his relative weakness and dreamy nature but – traditionally – he does. He comes good by virtue of his innate decency and open, childlike nature, or perhaps because he manages to enlist the help of a talking bird, who sets him on the path to victory. Even with help, the road he travels is not without its obstacles but, finally, after various tests, he brings home the prize – a pot of gold, say, or a beautiful princess – and, naturally, his brothers are jealous, resentful of his success and mystified as to how this little pipsqueak, this runt of any litter, could have succeeded where they had failed. And, of course, the youngest brother senses their anger, but forgives them anyway, and shares his good fortune, so that the story ends in concord, perhaps with a wedding, or unexpected kingship, or both. Most of all, what happens in the story causes changes in the Real World, where change of any kind is reason for hope. This is the best kind of story, because it is about a form of justice, tempered with mercy, that any child can appreciate.

As it happens, the story of the last Great Auk is not a traditional once-upon-a-time account. Instead, it is about three men who are not brothers, and the quest they are set is not only devoid of merit but also too banal to bring the victor glory – and maybe this is why everything is reversed in the telling. Here, the first two adventurers complete their task, while the third comes home empty-handed, and there is no kingship, no wedding, no happy ever after. True, the day-to-day world is changed by what happens, just as it is in the old stories, but that change is nothing that anyone would have wished for and, to begin with at least, it is barely noticed. In Jón Arason's kingdom, nobody knows what to make of it all, though several of the old folk seem to think that what has transpired is a bad omen – and this puts the narrative in an altogether different category. The category of warning. The category of cautionary tale. Like Hilaire Belloc's *Matilda: Who told Lies, and was Burned to Death*, or *Der Struwwelpeter* by Heinrich Hoffmann, a story that only the most hardened moraliser would read to a child.

It should be remembered, though, that human beings tell stories for all kinds of reasons. Some would say that it is our gift for storytelling that makes us unique amongst the animals, as if dolphins, or wolves, or bees, for that matter, had no stories to tell. Maybe that notion has become so widespread because we have drowned out so many of the other storytellers – and the quality of the biosphere's *vie commune* has suffered from that silencing. Now that we alone have the stage, the stories we tell are thinner, and less surprising. They ask less from us – they have become mere entertainments. A superhero with depressingly predictable powers averts yet another alien invasion. A pair of relatable dullards finds love against all odds in the big city, or the Deep South, or on some unlikely college campus. Like the old once-upon-a-time stories, Hollywood has its own menagerie of talking animals, but whenever they open their mouths they sound like teenagers from Los Angeles or Schenectady. Which, of course, they are.

What does make humans unique, however, is the fact that, no matter how many narratives we dream up to justify our sense of importance in a mysterious cosmos, we are the only creatures on earth who have too much to say. Unlike the wise old owl who lived in an oak, we speak, but we rarely listen; we tell cautionary tales, but we go on making the same mistakes; we state the obvious daily, yet we never act on what we say we know. Even at our dullest, we find ourselves a constant source of fascination. We choose our public figures for how forcefully they make arguments that we have heard a thousand times before, only to discover, the moment they take office, that it was all predictable lies. Celebrity is a false god, worldly success is an illusion, the cartoonish narratives we are spoon-fed are thumpingly obvious. If *Homo sapiens* is the storytelling species, then it seems more than a little sad that the tales we find so entertaining are so very banal.

And yet. And yet – at the same time, there are still narratives that go beyond the familiar chatter, stories that, when they come good, link us to one unfathomable, scintillant, never-ending tale: a tale that continues forever, beyond time and place, in the instantaneous, provisional, endlessly self-inventive realm of once-upon-a-time.

★

The last known pair of Great Auks (also known as Geirfugl, or Gairfowl) were killed on the 3rd of July 1844, on the island of Eldey, a basalt rock fifteen or so kilometres off the Reykjanes peninsula, in Western Iceland. Eldey, a volcanic outcrop populated only by seabirds, is composed of sheer cliffs on three sides, and it is small, just over a quarter of a kilometre square. Nowadays, it is prized by birdwatchers for its considerable gannet colony (around 16,000 pairs nest there in the early summer), but in the mid 1830s it was home to the last of Europe's Great Auks, who had moved in after their former home, another bare outcrop a few miles to the west, was obliterated in a volcanic eruption. By all accounts, that ancestral rock, Geirfuglasker, was fairly difficult to climb and, so, had been relatively safe from human predation (though those few hunting parties who did manage to ascend the rock made the most of their time there). Eldey, on the other hand, is accessible from one side, and that was the route taken, on that sub-Arctic summer's day in 1844, by three descendants of the bishop-poet, possible kinsmen who had been promised a modest fee to find and bring back a pair of adult Geirfugl for a museum collector. The men – Jón Brandsson, Sigurður Ísleifsson and Ketill Ketilsson – quickly found two nesting birds on the bare rocks, and caught them easily, as Ísleifsson told the British naturalist, John Wolley, fourteen years later:

> The [Auks] walked slowly. Jón Brandsson crept up with his arms open. The bird that Jón got went into a corner but [mine] was going to the edge of the cliff. It walked like a man ... but moved its feet quickly. [I] caught it close to the edge – a precipice many fathoms deep. Its wings lay close to the sides – not hanging out. I took him by the neck and he flapped his wings. He made no cry. I strangled him.

It should come as no surprise that Ísleifsson's account is matter-of-fact and unemotional; for him, taking the auks would have been just another day's work. Brandsson was also able to corner and kill his victim, but the third man, Ketilsson, who would later describe the Great Auks as 'incredible' and 'dignified', characterised his own part in that day's work in somewhat different terms. As he and the others crept up on the birds, he said, 'his head failed him', so that he not only failed to capture a specimen of his own, but also accidentally trod on the nest that the auks had been tending, thus rendering its single egg worthless to a collector.[31] In Wolley's account, he gives no further details, though it seems unlikely that his reaction was caused by any recognition that, in acting as they did, the men were driving a species to extinction. They had gone out that morning on just another hunting expedition, for a fee that would doubtless have provided a welcome supplement to their usual income. Nevertheless, Ketilsson was clearly moved by what he saw on Eldey, and the fact that he felt any qualms at all should mark him out as different from the others. Somehow, like the quest-hero in the old folk tales, he had sensed in these wild birds a quality that the others had missed, and this makes him the closest thing to a third brother in the scant, matter-of-fact account that Wolley and his travelling companion, Alfred Newton, brought back from Iceland, along with a few sad skeletal remains, in the summer of 1858.

That set of field notes and jottings is not a story, however. With a little work, it might be made into a cautionary tale, but what we find in Wolley's journals, other than Ketilsson's

---

31 As the birds had grown scarcer, due to hunting and feather-harvesting, so their eggs had become more valuable to collectors. Records show that, in 1832, a single egg was sold for around £16, almost double the average annual income for a skilled worker. by the 1890s, an auk's skin and a single egg was purchased for £630 (equivalent to around £82,000 today).

cryptic remark, is little more than a sketch: fourteen years earlier, three men travelled out on a summer's day to find specimen birds for a museum and, unwittingly, they destroyed the last of a species. Their actions are not uncommon for the time: all over the world, agents for museums and private collectors were sending local folk out into the wild to find animals, birds, eggs, feathers, skins, antlers, horns, rare butterflies, or new and previously unrecorded monkey, or snake, or beetle specimens. Collecting, whether for museums or for private individuals, could be a lucrative business. The entire animal was rarely shipped out whole, however. More often, the captured specimens would be skinned, or they would have their feathers stripped away, leaving the carcasses to rot in the snow or the desert scrub. Some hunters did not even bother to finish off their quarry, as this account, given in 1792 by an English sailor named Aaron Thomas reveals:

> If you come for their Feathers you do not give yourself the trouble of killing them, but lay hold of one and pluck the best of the Feathers. You then turn the poor [bird] adrift, with his skin half naked and torn off, to perish at his leasure. This is not a very humane method but it is the common practize.

Once they had been gathered in sufficient numbers, Great Auk feathers were used for quilts and bedding as an acceptable substitute for eiderdown (over hunting had almost eliminated the eider up and down the seacoast of North America by the late eighteenth century). When the birds were taken for museums, the skins were sent back to base, to be transformed, by skilled taxidermists, into rigid, inanimate likenesses of their former selves. Simulacra. All over the world, in museums and private collections, these lifeless figures stood in glass cases and alcoves, or lay packed into great wooden drawers, like the stuffed birds I once saw in the storeroom of Rome's zoological museum, glassy eyes staring, wings rigid, dead feet suspended in mid-air, as if trying to latch on to some branch or sea-splashed rock that was no longer there.

Few sights are more oppressive than the eerie stillness of taxidermy. A terrible stillness, a sense of awful interruption, gathers around a stuffed animal in a glass case or, worse, inserted into some facsimile of its natural habitat for a museum diorama. I have no wish to be unfair here – there is a strange beauty in the best examples of the taxidermist's art – but it is an oppressive beauty, nonetheless. It weighs on the heart, it crowds in upon the soul (if, by soul, we mean *anima*, the quality, not just of being alive, but of being responsive to, of being empathetic with, *la vie commune*). The argument can be made that these preserved likenesses have scientific and educational uses – and it is true that, confronted with a stuffed Great Auk, it is easier to appreciate how impressive the living bird would have been. At around eighty-five centimetres in height, and weighing approximately five kilograms, it was once the largest of the Alcidae, the family of seabirds that includes puffins, razorbills and guillemots, to which it bore some resemblance. The back, head and beak were black, and it had a white belly; during the summer months, patches of white plumage appeared around the eyes, a feature that changed gradually as the year progressed, to become a wider white band. Because of its size and colouring, seafarers tended to group it with the penguins: like its southern cousins, the Great Auk was flightless and, so, helpless on land. The stubby wings, barely fifteen centimetres in length, were adapted for swimming, not flight, and it was swift and agile in the water, a skilled hunter of Atlantic menhaden, capelin and crustaceans.

Great Auks lived for up to twenty-five years; though they built their nesting grounds in large colonies, each breeding couple mated for life. They would seem to have been unafraid of humans, which hastened their demise in such favoured haunts as Funk Island, a famed seabird colony around sixty kilometres from the Newfoundland coast, where George Cartwright noted, in 1785, that it had become customary:

> for several crews of men to live all summer on that island, for the sole purpose of killing birds for the sake of their feathers, the destruction which they have made is incredible. If a stop is not soon put to that practice, the whole breed will be diminished to almost nothing.

As we know, that warning went unheeded. Yet what is most striking about eyewitness accounts given by travellers who saw them at first hand is how often Great Auks are compared to humans. Sigurður Ísleifsson told John Wolley that the bird 'walked like a man' and other accounts give similar descriptions of the Auk's unique gait and manner. Perhaps the most vivid, and certainly the most poignant of these is a note in the journals of Christopher Almy, a whaler from New Bedford who describes a group of Gairfowl parading along a rocky northern shoreline as being 'like small boys a walking.' That said, it is no accident that this account should be given by a whaler – for, as much as collectors and museums must bear much of the blame for killing off the Great Auk, whaling played a significant role in driving the bird to extinction, not only by the actions of individual hunting parties from whale-boats, but also in the way the industry fostered a cold, entirely functional view of all living things, from the sperm whale to indigenous fishermen and, of course, to the seabirds they killed in the millions for food and fuel.

★

On a warm summer's day in 2001, I took the ferry from Gryllefjord, on Senja, to Andenes, an old fishing port on the northernmost tip of Andøya, in Norway's Vesterålen Islands. The short crossing was idyllic: the sea deep-blue, the sky cloudless, a host of different seabirds skimming over the boat, the merest glimpse of a whale off the bow. Finally, the forty-metre tall, red-painted Andenes lighthouse, which once guided fishing boats and whalers to safety, loomed overhead and, not two hours after departure, I was heading to the small village of Bleik, where I would be staying for a few days. Nowadays, the area has become more tourist-oriented than it was then, but in 2001, visitors mostly confined themselves to Andenes, where local boats offered whale-watching excursions and other attractions, and though I was only four miles away, I had the place mostly to myself. The cabin I had rented was right on Bleik's long white beach and so quiet that I heard nothing but the roll of the tide and the shore larks that flitted up and down the strand in the early mornings, when I would sit out with a pot of coffee and watch a group of sea eagles hunting in the wide, empty bay. It was a ritual they seemed to observe faithfully, each of them taking a turn to rise skyward over the deep-blue water then hovering, for the briefest of moments, before diving precipitously into the waves, only to rise seconds later with a bright, silvery fish in its beak. For me, those few days were bliss. While the great world ground by on its usual course, I had a chance to be still, to blend into the background, able to watch and listen, inclined towards healing.

This land was not always such a paradise, however. Turn the clock back to the later nineteenth century, when Andenes was a busy whaling station, and everything changes. The clear blue water is now cloudy and red, the surface slicked with whale oil, the water soured with spent flesh and dead matter – and on the air, the vile, gut-churning stink that Charles Nordhoff, an

American journalist who worked for a time on a whaling ship, singles out in an account he published in 1860:

> Everything is drenched with oil. Shirts and trowsers are dripping with the loathsome stuff. The pores of the skin seem to be filled with it. Feet, hands and hair, all are full. The biscuit you eat glistens with oil, and tastes as though just out of the blubber room. The knife with which you cut your meat leaves upon the morsel, which nearly chokes you as you reluctantly swallow it, plain traces of the abominable blubber. Every few minutes it becomes necessary to work at something on the lee side of the vessel, and while there you are compelled to breath in the fetid smoke of the scrap fires, until you feel as though filth had struck into your blood, and suffused every vein in your body. From this smell and taste of blubber, raw, boiling and burning, there is no relief or place of refuge.

Today, when we think of whaling, we tend to imagine the cold brutality of the modern hunt[32], a highly-industrialised process in which a magnificent, obviously intelligent mammal is slaughtered with a grenade-like harpoon that does not explode until it has penetrated ten to twelve inches into the flesh. In the mid-to-late nineteenth century, however, when the whale trade was booming, the slaughter was more plentiful and, potentially, even more cruel.

Meanwhile, for those who lived in and around whaling harbours across the world, there had always been a massive impact – not least from the stench of waste blubber, blood and offal discarded by the factory ships – on the quality of day-to-day existence. Many whalers began the work of processing their catch at sea, but it was not uncommon for

---

32 Setting aside allowances made for traditional indigenous whalers in several countries, only Norway, Japan, and Iceland currently engage in the commercial pursuit of large whales.

part-butchered carcasses to be hauled close to shore, where it was easier to cut away the unwanted flesh and complete not just the harvest of blubber, which would be boiled down in large copper cauldrons to extract the oil, but also to harvest other raw materials, such as baleen (used in corsets and skirt-hoops) ambergris (an ingredient of high-end perfumes) and the highly-prized spermaceti (a waxy substance extracted from the whale's head) from which high-quality candles were manufactured. The main product, however, was oil, which came in varying grades and forms, and was used for lighting, in textile, soap and paint manufacturing and as a lubricant in every kind of mechanical device, from guns and clocks to industrial plant. By the middle of the nineteenth century, whaling was a highly lucrative business; records show that, by the early 1850s, the industry was worth around $11 million dollars in the United States alone, making the town of New Bedford, Massachusetts, one of the world's wealthiest cities, per capita. Not surprisingly, seafarers and adventurers from across America began fetching up in the New England sea-towns, hoping to cash in. According to Herman Melville, however, the best whalers came from island communities like Shetland and The Azores:

> No small number of these whaling seamen belong to the Azores, where the outward bound Nantucket whalers frequently touch to augment their crews from the hardy peasants of those rocky shores. In like manner, the Greenland whalers sailing out of Hull or London, put in at the Shetland Islands, to receive the full complement of their crew. Upon the passage homewards, they drop them there again. How it is, there is no telling, but Islanders seem to make the best whalemen.

Like all boom industries, whaling was very profitable for a few, while offering others a means, not only of subsistence but also 'a way ... of driving off the spleen and regulating the circulation.' Yet it also degraded coastal communities the world over, leading to unrest and even rioting amongst locals, who objected, not only to the pollution of their waters and the disruption of fish stocks, but also to gross environmental impacts on the sea, land and air caused by industrial-scale whaling.

Meanwhile, the industry was creating a class of rootless men who travelled the seas, working under considerable duress in locations that felt not a bit like home. When they were hungry, they hunted for food, and the easier the prey, the better. This took its toll on local species wherever they went, especially on flightless birds like the penguin, in southern waters, and on Great Auk populations from Newfoundland to the Norway coast. It should come as no surprise that, for men who were no more than cogs in a ruthless international industry – men who mostly belonged to nowhere in particular, risking life and limb to fill the coffers of rich merchants in New Bedford and Nantucket – the Great Auks they encountered in their voyages across the Atlantic rim should have been nothing more than meat. Easy pickings. Records show that, as late as Shackleton's 1914 voyage to Antarctica, southern sailors hunted for penguins; in the north, however, the Great Auk was not only pursued for food, but was even exploited as a fuel source, as Aaron Thomas observes:

> While you abide on this island you are in the constant practize of horrid cruelties for you not only skin them Alive, but you burn them Alive also to cook their Bodies with. You take a kettle with you into which you put a [bird] or two, you kindle a fire under it, and this fire is absolutely made of the unfortunate [birds] themselves. Their bodys being oily soon produce a Flame; there is no wood on the island.

What is striking, here, is how keenly aware Thomas is of the cruelty that he and his fellow sailors are inflicting on birds that, unable to fly to safety, and fatally trusting of humanity, were entirely helpless. And yet, the cruelty continued. Even when Great Auk populations fell into visible decline, the slaughter went on unabated. Finally, when there was almost nothing left, the skins, eggs and plumage became status symbols for gentlemen collectors, who paid good money, and were prepared to go to extreme lengths, to obtain the last existing specimens of this dying tribe. In the new age of industry, even that harvest was ruthless and efficient – as was the needless waste. When Ketill Ketilsson's boot came down on the last known Great Auk's egg, the fatal moment epitomises the entire story of humans and Auks, a story of profligacy, arrogance and a casual disregard for life that, when taken into anything like due consideration, is almost impossible to fathom.

Selected excerpts from *The Great Auk, or Garefowl*, a paper read before the members of the Hastings and St Leonards Natural History Society on June 28, 1894, by Thomas Parkin M.A.

> In this age it seems singular that ornithologists should not have sooner anticipated [The Great Auk's] destruction and that absolutely no precautionary measures were taken to check the senseless slaughter to which it was, through its incapacity of flight, subjected. Much of the strangeness, however, will disappear when we consider the fact that the Garefowl became extinct in an age when interest in birds was not so widespread as it now is; and especially when we bear in mind that the bird was unfortunate enough to be a desired article of food, and an easy prey.

Mr. Seebohm says, 'It was once a British bird; now it is regarded as an extinct species, like the Solitaire Pigeon of Rodriguez, the Phillip-Island Parrot, the Dodo of the Mauritius, and the Moa of New Zealand. The extinction of the Great Auk has taken place during the lifetime of the present generation. It is scarcely more than half a century since the last British example of this curious bird was killed in the Orkneys; and when, ten years later, the survivors of the only colony left were captured, the history of the Great Auk became a legend of the past.'

...

According to descriptions by early writers it would appear that the Garefowls sat in a position even more erect than that of our common Guillemot (Uria troile, L.) or Razor-Bill (Alca torda, L.) but chose a breeding place farther from the water. Unusual noises frightened them; but they appeared insensible to strange sights, or treated them with absolute disregard. The only vocal capabilities of the bird extended to the production of sundry low croaks. They walked or ran with quick short steps. They appear to have been extremely stupid, and also insatiate in their appetites.

...

A Great Auk was killed at Papa Westray, Orkneys, by some fishermen, who enticed it within reach by offering fish, and then killed it with an oar.

...

Audubon mentions the capture of a Great Auk by the brother of his engraver, while on a voyage from New York to England. He says, 'The bird was hooked, and on being hauled on board it was left at liberty on deck; it walked very awkwardly, often tumbling over, bit every one within reach of its powerful bill, and refused food of all kinds. After continuing several days on board it was restored to its proper element.'

...

In Hakluyt's voyages, edited 1600, we find the earliest mention of the Great Auk or Penguin (the two names were often misapplied) and in the description of a voyage to Newfoundland and Cape Breton in 1536 mention is made of the Island of Penguins, and that, 'they found it full of great fowls, white and grey, and big as geese, and they saw infinite numbers of their eggs.' The first account of this extraordinary bird as a British species is that given by M. Martin in a curious little book entitled 'A voyage to St. Kilda, the remotest of all the Hebrides.' Martin thus describes the birds, 'The Sea Fowls are first the Gairfowl, being the stateliest, as well as the largest of the fowls here, and about the size of a Solan Goose; of a black colour, red about the eyes, a large white spot under each, a long broad bill; stands stately, its whole body erected, its wing short, it flieth not at all, lays its eggs upon a bare rock, which if taken away it layeth no more that year.'

...

About the latter end of the fifteenth century a war of extermination was waged against the Garefowls, and continued until scarcely any were left. Ships engaged in the fisheries off Newfoundland were provisioned with them, as they proved a valuable article of food. Their stupidity when on land was so great that they allowed themselves to be driven on board over planks and sails spread out from the sides of the ship to the shore. In spite, however of the destruction which had so long gone on, and so greatly diminished their numbers, it was not thought that the species was coming to an end, and it was not in fact until the thirties in the present century that the 'first note of warning was sounded' which came from a writer in a Danish Journal, who in 1838 predicted the extinction of the bird. Six years later the Great Auk had ceased to exist.

...

A male and female were killed in 1812 at. Papa Westray one of the Orkneys. The female although knocked over by some boys with stones, was not obtained until afterwards washed ashore. Mr. Bullock states that he caused the male to be chased for several hours; but, although the boat was manned by six swift rowers, the chase had to be abandoned on account of the amazing velocity of the bird through the water. It was killed soon after, by some fishermen who sent the body to Mr. Bullock.

...

It was at the now submerged Geirfuglasker that there occurred the greatest slaughter of the birds. It appears that this colony had several times been in danger of extermination, as the descents that were made on this particular skerry have been well recorded. The first of these was perpetrated by the crew of a privateer named the Salamine, commanded by John Gilpin. They visited the Garefowl skerry, and remained a whole day, killing many birds and trampling down their eggs. Similar descents succeeded. In 1813 the inhabitants of the Faroes were in an almost starving condition, and while a ship with provisions, sent to their relief, was becalmed off Geirfuglasker, advantage was taken of the occasion to visit the skerry. The crew killed all the birds they could lay their hands on, and among the slain were many Auks.

★

All that needless slaughter must have been exhausting – and yet, at various points during these adventures in extermination, attempts were made to conserve the Great Auk. Because the main depredations were initially caused by hunters collecting down, bans were put in place in Britain and Canada during the late eighteenth century, in an attempt to control the mass slaughter of birds for their feathers. Punishment ranged from fines to public flogging, but the new laws were impossible to enforce when so much of the killing happened on remote skerries and islands across the Atlantic rim or in the sub-Arctic, far from any effective jurisdiction. Meanwhile, sheer stupidity and superstition played their part in local extirpations of the Gairfowl. In 1840, just four years before the last Auk was killed on Eldey, a group of locals on St Kilda's Stac an Armin discovered a single bird roosting on the rocks, captured it and brought it to a nearby bothy, where they kept it prisoner for three days. What their intentions in imprisoning the creature might have been, we do not know, but on the third day a great storm blew in and, convinced that the Auk was a witch in disguise, they killed it. Whether the storm then lifted is not on the record; what does seem clear, however, is that those involved did not even know what it was they were killing.

And so it was that, for a variety of reasons, none of them very honourable, *Homo sapiens*, a thinking, story-telling, highly-skilled primate, killed off *Pinguinus impennis*, a flightless bird whose movements were poignantly reminiscent of 'small boys a walking'. Greed, necessity, folly and superstition all played their part, though in practical terms, the Great Auk was simply hunted to death because it was fairly easy to catch. First it was killed because the plumage supplied an acceptable substitute for eider which, by the end of the eighteenth century, had itself been harvested close to the point of extinction; then it was used as a convenient source of food and live fuel by whalers and other seafarers until, finally, when numbers fell so low that it acquired a scarcity value, its eggs and skins were coveted by gentlemen collectors in European and American cities. Perhaps the best summary of the relationship between humans and the Gairfowl, however, is provided by Sir Richard Whitbourne, sea captain and colonist, who, in 1622, gave genteel expression to a certain brand of manifest entitlement in his elaborately titled *A discourse and discouery of Nevv-found-land with many reasons to prooue how worthy and beneficiall a plantation may there be made, after a far better manner than now it is. Together with the laying open of certaine enormities and abuses commited by some that trade to that countrey, and the meanes laide downe for reformation thereof*:

> These Penguins are as big as geese . . . and they multiply so infinitely upon a certain flat island that men drive them from hence upon a board, into their boat by the hundreds at a time, *as if God had made the innocencie of so poor a creature to become such an admirable instrument for the sustenation of man*. [my italic]

Blossom: Ruins

It started with the bats. For some time they had been flitting back and forth around my head, before darting out to the far corners of the room where, suspecting I had Covid-19, I was self-isolating, surrounded by books I couldn't read, soothed by music that, as my mind wandered ever further into the far recesses of CO^2 intoxication, seemed to be coming, spontaneously, out of nowhere. Maybe it was – all my memories of that time are both luminous and so vague that it is difficult, now, to describe the condition into which I had fallen. The bats seemed altogether real and yet, now and then, even as I saw and felt them flicker past my head, a last shred of common sense would start into life to question their reality. At other times, I would detach, somehow, into fleeting, but utterly lucid moments of supreme clarity, during which I would begin to suspect that my self-diagnosis was wrong. Yes, difficulty breathing. Yes, fever, if my disorientated state was anything to go by. Yes, a dry, intermittent cough – but then, was that a defined Covid symptom? I never did work that one out: all I knew was that something wasn't right, and then, in an instant, I was lost again, following the bats as they beat to and fro, dark wings brushing the walls. It was April 30, 2020. The Eve of Beltane. Walpurgisnacht.

The festival days of the old Celtic year – Samhain (now Halloween, or All Saints' Day), Imbolc (Candlemas), Beltane

(Mayday) and Lughnasadh (Lammas) – are not quite extinct. Instead, they have been consigned to what the poet and folklorist, Lewis Spence, calls Faerie, which:

> represents a species of limbo, a great abyss of traditional material, into which every kind of ancient belief came to be cast as the acceptance of one new faith after another dictated the abandonment of forms and ideas unacceptable to its doctrines ...[33]

For Spence, the post-Celtic idea of Faerie came about as a clearing house, so to speak, for the powerful and stubborn gods of the old religion, who adhered to the land and refused to go away on their own. When Christianity overtook pagan Europe, the practice was, not to try to expunge the old gods altogether, but to turn them into saints (for example, the Celtic Brigit, goddess of spring, poetry, healing and holy wells, becomes the rather insipid but extremely charitable St Brigid, who was said to have lived an exemplary Christian life in spite of having been born into a pagan community). If canonisation was impractical, the *genii* of the land were marginalised in the dim bourn of old wives' tales and superstition where, instead of being sources of inspiration and connection to the natural world, they became bogeymen to be scared off or dismissed as fantastical:

> At Bealltainn, or May Day, every effort was made to scare away the fairies, who were particularly dreaded at this season. In the West Highlands charms were used to avert their influence. In the Isle of Man the gorse was set alight to keep them at a distance. In some parts of Ireland the house was sprinkled with holy water to ward off fairy influence. These are only a mere handful out of the large number of references available, but they seem to me to reveal an effort to

---

[33] Lewis Spence, *British Fairy Origins*, Watts and Co, London, 1946.

avoid the attentions of discredited deities on occasions of festival once sacred to them. The gods duly return at the appointed season, but instead of being received with adoration, they are rebuffed by the descendants of their former worshippers, who have embraced a faith which regards them as demons.[34]

By such strategies, Christianity sought to diminish and marginalise those powers in the land that they could not kill outright. Thus, as Spence suggests: 'in all likelihood fairies of larger stature were ancient gods in a state of decay', while the tolerance of the old holy rituals, now repurposed as saints' days, or hokey festivals like Halloween or Walpurgisnacht, allowed for the gradual demotion of real elementals to the level of witches, demons and sprites:

> On the conversion of the European tribes to Christianity the ancient pagan worship was by no means incontinently abandoned. So wholesale had been the conversion of many peoples, whose chiefs or rulers had accepted the new faith on their behalf in a summary manner, that it would be absurd to suppose that any general acquiescence in the new gospel immediately took place. Indeed, the old beliefs lurked in many neighbourhoods, and even a renaissance of some of them occurred in more than one area. Little by little, however, the Church succeeded in rooting out the public worship of the old pagan deities, but it found it quite impossible to effect an entire reversion of pagan ways, and in the end compromised by exalting the ancient deities to the position of saints in its calendar, either officially, or by usage. In the popular mind, however, these remained as the fairies of woodland and stream, whose worship in a broken-down form still flourished at wayside wells and forest shrines. The Matres, or Mother gods, particularly

---

34 ibid

those of Celtic France and Ireland, the former of
which had come to be Romanized, became the *bonnes
dames* of folklore, while the *dusii* and *pilosi*, or hairy
house-sprites, were so commonly paid tribute that
the Church introduced a special question concerning
them into its catechism of persons suspected of
pagan practice. Nevertheless, the Roman Church,
at a somewhat later era, reversed its older and more
catholic policy, and sternly set its face against the
cultus of paganism in Europe, stigmatizing the several
kinds of spirits and derelict gods who were the objects
of its worship as demons and devils, whom mankind
must eschew with the most pious care if it were to
avoid damnation.[35]

In literature, these liminal days offer rich characters and dramatic incidents for poets and dramatists to work with – the most famous example being Goethe's depiction of Walpurgisnacht in Book One of *Faust*, where Mephistopheles introduces his protégé to a grotesque parade of witches, demons and succubi. The scene is at once threatening and darkly comical, but by the end it has become too wild even for Mephistopheles:

> Here, doctor, grasp me! With a single bound
> Let us escape this ceaseless jar;
> Even for me too mad these people are.
> Hard by there shineth something with peculiar glare,
> Yon brake allureth me; it is not far;
> Come, come along with me! we'll slip in there.[36]

This is what remains of the old Celtic Beltane in the Age of Enlightenment: a realm of semi-comical nightmare visions and vulgar superstitions. A feast of the grotesque and the

---

35   ibid
36   Goethe: Faust, tr. Anna Swanwick (1909) P.F. Collier & Son, NY.

vulgar. An absurd demonarchy. Even at a distance from the old ways that one informed pagan life in Europe, it is clear that Goethe's outlandish visions bear no resemblance, and do a severe injustice to that way of life – but then, as with so many such movements, the great European Enlightenment seems to have been unreasonably hostile to the old ways, and could only rest when, through a process of wilful travesty and misrepresentation, it had reduced all the magic in the world to the level of wilful fraud or laughable superstition.

During my personal, bat-haunted Walpurgisnacht, however, I had become entangled in a more modern variety of superstitious thinking, following a trail of assumptions, internet queries, anecdotal evidence and pseudoscience to where I now sat, in makeshift quarantine, waiting for something that wasn't real to pass. I was fighting for breath, any physical activity was an effort, I had been suffering for weeks from a dry, nagging cough and, though these could have been symptoms of anything, from a common cold, through bronchitis, to the unforeseen combination of 'co-morbidities' that, over the next several days, almost killed me, I had resolved upon Corona. Self-diagnosis, followed by self-medication: as with so many men my age, it was infinitely preferable to seeing a doctor.

Though as it happened, I *had* considered calling my GP – but that would have led straight to A&E and, as everybody knows, more people get sick in hospital than they would have done, had they stayed home. Besides, what could a hospital do for me? There was no vaccine, and no treatment, other than rest and rehydration. If things got significantly worse, I told myself, I could call the Hotline tomorrow. For now, though, the idea of self-isolation felt, not only appropriate, but also, in a perverse way, aesthetically pleasing, like the idea of sanctuary, or monastic contemplation. If I stayed comfortable and warm at home, I would probably come through fine; if I didn't, I at least had my own books and music to hand. After all, who can forget George Herbert's epigram: 'The Apothecary's mortar spoils the luter's music.' Better to die in my own bed than on a hospital ward, surrounded by people I didn't know, and with the possibility of muzak, or worse, a TV soap, as the soundtrack to my demise.

Luckily, my wife disagreed. Breaking into my 'quarantine', she found a grey-faced spectre, gasping for every breath, and in a thoroughly confused state, (I was told later that the build-up of carbon dioxide in my blood was the reason, not only for my bat hallucinations, but also for the sequence of bad decisions that had brought me to this point). I can be pig-headed, especially in adversity, and for a while she had tried to see my point of view; now, however, as I drifted ever further from reality, she picked up the phone. Within an hour, the ambulance had brought me to A&E and, because of my laboured breathing, I was quickly whisked into the 'Red Zone', which is to say, to the Covid-19 side of the building. From here on in, there was no going back. I had entered a parallel state, with its own arcane procedures, in a super-sanitised limbo where everything was muffled and several degrees removed, like a world under water. For the next six days, I would meet any number of people, but none of them would have faces, and their voices would be stifled and distant. Later, it would come as a surprise that I got used to this so quickly; on that first day, however, it was decidedly eerie and, given my mental state, insanely cinematic. As soon as I arrived, the staff gathered around me and, as they poked and prodded and adjusted my oxygen supply, they looked like curious, oversized insects in their masks and visors: bees, say, or ants. (This never changed, even when I got the Covid all-clear: in all my time at the hospital, I never got to see the people who effectively saved my life; all I saw was a series of PPE exoskeletons and, excepting their first names, all I knew about them was the sound of their muffled voices.)

If the medical staff were ants, however, the Red Zone exposed me as another form of insect life altogether. My family had been nagging me for years about my weight, but I had refused to acknowledge the problem, right up until that definitive moment, when three nurses rolled me from the gurney on to a bed and I saw myself, from the outside, as a damp, larval mass, a fat, overblown grub in which, deep down, a thin reddish glimmer represented all that remained of my original élan vital. That came as a shock, though it shouldn't have done. I had 'let myself go' over years, my time divided between my desk and various forms of transport, my diet an ad-hoc, pro-tem mix of cheese sandwiches, stale *vol-au-vents* and official dinners. Junk food and midnight snacks. Double helpings when the food was good (or very bad); lashings of whipped cream; disturbing quantities of energy drinks and black coffee. No alcohol, though. After being diagnosed with severe sleep problems (and following a couple of embarrassing incidents resulting from a combination of sleeplessness and even moderate quantities of wine) I had abruptly gone teetotal – and this had been enough for me to convince myself that I could improve. Later, when there was time, I would *do something*. I might even go on one of those Well-Being courses at work. Or start swimming again, maybe. For now, though, I was far too *busy*.

After admission, my memories of the first night are confused. Everyone was talking at once. One of the ants was trying to get me to blow into a device that looked like a breathalyser, others were already fitting me with a drip of some kind, while a tiny, Tinkerbelle-like creature floated around the periphery of my vision, waiting to insert what I would soon realise was a catheter. This all seemed to be happening at once, a makeshift theatre of managed chaos, like a scene from *Casualty* or an alien abduction movie. Then, just as suddenly, it was quiet. I may have drifted briefly into unconsciousness, but I can't be certain; all I can say is that, at one cold and very still moment, I rose vaguely to the surface, caught my breath and listened. No-one was there. Apparently, I had been abandoned.

By now, the bats were everywhere; though, admittedly, this was far less troubling than it sounds. A survivor of the 1970s, I remain highly tolerant of hallucinations, even those on the grislier side. These bats weren't grisly at all, however; they were just haunting and oddly poignant, as they fluttered against the walls, searching for an exit. For one dizzy moment, I thought that I might be able to lift myself out of bed and follow them; but then I saw that, in spite of their best efforts, they weren't going anywhere. There *was* no exit; or not, at least, anything that could be seen from where I was lying, no longer a larval mass, just an overweight, utterly extenuated human male in late middle-age. Of course, I couldn't see the entire room because, like Gulliver in Lilliput, I was pinned down by an elaborate system of tubes and wiring. The ants might have abandoned me, but they had tethered my body to a variety of monitors and drips and bleeping instruments, and I was still being fed oxygen through a large, clear face mask – which suggested that, at some point, somebody would turn up to do whatever remained to be done. For the time being, however, I was alone, and the sealed room was quiet. It was a veritable study in solipsism: I existed, I was sentient, but nothing else was certain. Finally, I closed my eyes, deliberately this time, and with something close to grim satisfaction, like Lazarus, I departed.

There is no time in the Red Zone, so I am only guessing when I assume that it must have been around then that the doctor telephoned my wife, soliciting her agreement that, if I continued on my present path, they would not attempt CPR or put me on a ventilator. (Apparently, my particular combination of 'co-morbidities' – which is to say, the simultaneous presence of two or more potentially fatal conditions in the same patient – meant that such measures would only prolong the misery.) This she reluctantly did. Not surprisingly, she had more questions to ask, but the person who had called had no ready answers, other than to advise her to 'prepare for the worst.' For the moment, they would keep me on oxygen, but if I didn't start breathing independently, I would die. I only learned all this later, however, after I had made it through the first stage of recovery. For now, I was on the other side of sleep, in what Dylan Thomas calls 'the close and holy darkness.' I have no memory of those lost hours, and none of the visions commonly reported by near-death patients. What I do recall is that, when I emerged, I felt an odd detachment, a sense of peace that I wouldn't even have attempted to explain. I want to say that this was by no means a religious, or even a 'spiritual' experience; on the contrary, it was altogether this-worldly. Earthly. Natural. A perfect instance, in fact, of *blossomiest blossom*.

To fans of television drama, that reference may sound familiar. It comes from an interview Dennis Potter gave in 1994, during which he remarked: 'The only thing you know for sure is the present tense, and that nowness becomes so vivid that, almost in a perverse sort of way, I'm almost serene. You know, I can celebrate life.' By that stage, he was close to death, his pain muted with morphine, but he appeared to be as clear-headed as ever. He continued: 'Below my window in Ross … the blossom is out in full now … It's a plum tree, it looks like apple blossom but it's white, and looking at it ... I see it is the whitest, frothiest, *blossomiest blossom* that there ever could be, and I can see it. Things are both more trivial than they ever were, and more important than they ever were, and the difference between the trivial and the important doesn't seem to matter. But the nowness of everything is absolutely wondrous.'

I remember that, back then, the phrase *blossomiest blossom* stuck in my mind, not just for its dubious grammar, but because it seemed to capture a sensation that I had experienced, off and on, since childhood, a sensation that is equally well-expressed, albeit in more theoretical form, by Wittgenstein's notion of *das Mystische* in proposition 6.44 of the *Tractatus Logico-Philosophicus*: 'It is not how things are in the world that is mystical, but *that it exists*' (my italics). I have no great wish to get into philosophy here; rather, I find myself, not for the first time, in pursuit of something that cannot be expressed in logical terms. Nevertheless, it does seem important, for several reasons, not least ecosophical, that one of philosophy's more interesting aims, during the last century, was to strip away the religious paraphernalia from *das Mystische* and express it as an earthly, quotidian experience, while still retaining Potter's intuition of 'the wondrous.' Of course, writing this now, I am painfully aware that it is all entirely theoretical, an obvious and fairly cack-handed attempt to give voice to 'that whereof one cannot speak.' Yet what mattered, at that moment in the hospital, when I returned, Lazarus-like, from the far side of sleep, was the *feeling* I had – a kind of detachment, yes, but a responsive detachment tempered with a real sense of wonder and the impulse, as Potter puts it, to celebrate life. I don't know how long I lay there, alone – maybe minutes, maybe longer. During that time, I became aware that somebody had been to tidy me up: where the sheets had been rucked and damp with sweat before, the smooth, freshly-laundered bedcovers now confined me perfectly. It also seemed that my face had been washed or, at the very least, lightly swabbed with some sweet-scented lotion or soap. For a moment, I was confused. Had this been done as part of some formal ritual, because I was dying, or was it related in some way to Covid-19? Clearly, I still wasn't thinking straight; and yet I felt calm, detached from my own predicament, even slightly bemused, not least by the questions that were running through my head. Looking back, I see that this wandering and utterly trivial chain of questions might have gone on indefinitely, leaving me forever suspended in time and place. Luckily, however, a nurse arrived, bearing strange, yet entirely predictable gifts.

I suppose every return from great injury or mortal terror contains a spell – an hour, a day, a long moment – when some hitherto banal event becomes highly poignant, a landmark in the heart's geography. There is no way to explain why this ordinary event seems to hold some improbable yet oddly inevitable meaning; all we can do is grasp it when it comes, like Ariadne's thread, and hope that it will lead us back to the known world, a little wiser, a little lighter, a little more appreciative of everyday blessings than before. Humbler, it should go without saying, though in no way diminished. In this case, what led me back was a tomato sandwich on white bread, and a cup of very weak, very milky tea. It's hardly a poetic image, yet there was something about its very banality that delighted me. To begin with, I was quite sceptical about the whole process – could I actually eat this? Would I ever be able to eat food again? After some hesitation, however, and with a little help from the nurse, I managed to consume my – what? Lunch? dinner? I had no idea what time, or even what day of the week it was. And all I know now is that nothing I have ever eaten has tasted so wonderful – and it probably goes without saying that, as long as I have breath, I will treat every tomato sandwich that life offers me with nothing less than the fullest sense of *blossomiest blossom*.

It was the taste of that sandwich, which I ate very slowly, and with considerable relish, that convinced me that I wasn't going to die quite yet. The next several days were, by turns, wonderfully solitary and strangely convivial; the nurses and doctors who came and went were clearly surprised (and, apparently, rather pleased) that I had come through more or less intact (as one nurse observed, when I thanked him for some kindness, there was no need for thanks, he was just happy to see me getting better – and I was reminded that, for these people, in this long season of 'excess deaths', even a partial success story had to have been some kind of blessing). I will admit, now, that I held these people in real, and rather sentimental awe, though I was mostly tongue-tied at the time, rendered awkward and speechless by the enormity of what they were doing, for me and for others, on a daily basis. And, like many of those who have stood at their front doors every week to applaud our NHS 'heroes', I wanted to thank every nurse and porter and auxiliary I encountered for their unstinting kindness and professionalism but, all too obviously, this is not what is needed. What is needed is fair pay and decent working conditions, not virtual haloes and angels' wings. The absurd discrepancies in remuneration between these essential workers, people of real value in a crisis, and those who spend their lives engineering environmental and human crises for profit have been obvious for years – and I remember wishfully thinking that, if one thing were to come out of the pandemic, it should be justice for all of those who keep the actual world, not only running, but more merciful than it would be otherwise. My brush with mortality might have chastened me, but this was significantly less humbling than the care I was given by everyone from the paramedics who got me to A&E on time, to the exhausted junior doctors who seemed never to leave the wards, to the nurses who, quite literally, kept me breathing. Nobody can say that these people are as culpable as the CEOs and politicos who keep the extinction machinery running – they, at least, have chosen to work on the side of life. This should not be forgotten. We are by no means *all in this together* – and we never were. I say again: this should not be forgotten.

Six days after I was supposed to die, my wife came to the hospital door to ferry me home – and though I had only been gone a week, everything had changed. Suddenly, in the yards and gardens that lined the road, it was summer; the street trees were leafing up and, here and there on the new estates, a Japanese cherry, or a flowering almond, stood resplendent in its own tight plot of emerald lawn. One, in particular, caught my eye, a blowsy, spreading 'Shirofugen' cherry that immediately brought Potter's *blossomiest blossom* remark to mind. I had driven this road often, but it had never looked so beautiful. At the same time, because the journey was slow, in spite of the lockdown, I had time to revisit a game I had played as a child, peering through the window of my uncle's car at the passing streets and imagining what it was like to live in one of those houses, to walk across this farmyard at first light, to sleep with another in that upper room. In a poem from 1917, ('During Wind and Rain') Thomas Hardy describes a family's life over a period of years, mixing elegy with matter-of-fact celebration, as they create their first home with 'pathways neat / and the garden gay' until finally, as the poem ends, they

> change to a high new house, He, she, all of them—aye,
> Clocks and carpets and chairs
> On the lawn all day,
> And brightest things that are theirs...
> Ah, no; the years, the years;
> Down their carved names the rain-drop ploughs.

The ambiguity in this last stanza is masterly: given that final image of rain-ploughed headstones, we may imagine that 'new high house' as an afterlife (perhaps, though not necessarily, the Christian heaven) and so picture a continuity that runs beyond the actors' mortal span. With characteristic economy, Hardy sums up the joys and losses of an entire generation in just four seven-line stanzas, carefully balancing images of light and dark, growth and decay, work and leisure, destruction and making, the mystery of distance with domestic intimacy. Life ends, he suggests, and most people make no great mark in history, but they live, in community, and they find *blossomiest blossom* moments amidst that flux – moments that do not last, in linear time, but somehow endure in the fabric of *das Mystische*, which is to say: the common miracle (and highly unlikely fact) of presence where, as John Ashbery has noted

> life is divided up
> Between you and me, and among all the others out
> there.

I tell this story, partly because the events described seem, after the fact, to have connected me in some manner to the vitally endangered, but not extinct life of a pagan past that has been thoroughly and wilfully clouded by the religion in which, as an impressionable child, I was raised to credit superstitions that struck me, even then, as far more irrational than anything my several churches have consigned to the dustbin of history. For a short time, that trip to the Red Zone, bats and all, connected me to the deeper roots of *la vie commune* – and I have come to see the bats that circled me in my non-Covid fugue state, not as hangovers from a childhood dedicated to Hammer Horror movies and ghost stories, but as something more companionable – even as familiar spirits or totem creatures that temporarily emerged from the limbo of the old, pagan Europe, if not to heal, then at least to guide me. Why these familiars took the form of bats, I do not know. I would probably have preferred a flock of starlings, or a charm of goldfinches – but what I suspect happened was that, as the CO_2 clouded my brain, I began to experience anomalies in the flow of information from my retina to my visual cortex, which I then transformed imaginatively to their nearest likenesses. However, this suggestion is not intended as an explanation – or at least, not in the sense of *explaining away*. The bats did not come into being *as bats* because of a chemical anomaly in my eyes or my brain, and there is no *away* here. What I saw, physically, was a set of black shapes and patterns which I elaborated into a very realistic flock of bats – but that is not the end of the matter. Following that elaboration, I then interpreted my visions as familiars and drew from them a meaning that, for me, was quite separate from brain chemistry and the question of where hallucinations come from. At that moment bats fulfilled a necessary role, and possibly what remained of a sacred function, just as the sacred aurochs did for members of the Mithras cult, or the Cretan bull-dancers. The actual history and meaning of my own animist memories may be open to argument, and I am not about to erect a shrine to

The Sacred Bat in my back yard but, as easy as it might be to concur with the reductive orthodoxy of the age, I continue unpersuaded that the chemistry of the brain accounts entirely and conclusively for the life of the mind – a phenomenon that finds its full expression, not in an individual cerebellum, but out there, in the constant play of *la vie commune*.

The other reason for retelling an event that occupies the grey area between delirium and the territory normally covered by near-death narratives, popular media anecdotes of reincarnation and the Tibetan Book of the Dead, is the fact that it brought home to me a strong physical sense of the basic existential fact that what is, passes. Just as firmly as I trust in *la vie commune*, I tend to the belief that each of us who is, or has been here on earth, is destined for inexistence. Each of us will become an instance of what has been and will not be again and that fact is rather poignant. At the same time, there is something intrinsically interesting, or perhaps useful, to be gleaned from any brush with the Grim Reaper. Behind every near-death experience (and behind every death) there is a story of some kind and, though some of those stories, when told in the light of day, end up sounding like clichés or flights of fancy, others come across as persuasive, at the very least, and they help to frame certain questions – not ideas so much as brief, but vivid intuitions – about how mortality works. It is inviting to settle for the most basic set of existential propositions – we are born, we live as well as circumstances allow, and we die – but anyone who has entered the realm of Blossomiest Blossom, however briefly, comes away with a sense that there is more to being here than that. At the fundamental, experiential level, the near-death encounter confirms C.G. Jung's argument that:

The unconscious has no time. There is no trouble about time in the unconscious. Part of our psyche is not in time and not in space. They are only an illusion, time and space, and so in a certain part of our psyche time does not exist at all.

Yet there is even more to the Blossomiest Blossom state than this – for what it also brings is a sensation of being, not wholly separate and individuated, and not even connected to some lattice-like whole, but of being continuous with the entire fabric of *la vie commune*. A sensation, that is, of total belonging, at least in the Dreamtime, that has nothing to do with religion, or faith, or choice, but is simply a sensation that, like profound pain, blank fear or the immense peace that comes of detachment from individual concerns, is too immediate to refute, even as it is too intractable to objective thinking to express in non-lyrical speech.

Before I entered the Red Zone, I was a devotee of Near-Death Experience (NDE) stories. I did not see them as proof of anything, I just enjoyed hearing or reading them. Hearing is best – in spoken accounts, the tone of voice is often warm, generous and reverent, even amongst those who do not see their experience as divine or otherworldly – but that tone can also shine through in print. At the same time, though I am mildly interested in knowing more about the chemistry of such events (for example, researchers have found that, in rats, serotonin levels rise threefold at the point of death) what seems more interesting is the long-term effect on a subject who 'survives' a near-death event. Executive Director at the Karma Collaborative, Alana Karran suggests that accounts of NDEs are:

similar to the hero's journey, or quest narrative, the structure that the American writer and mythologist Joseph Campbell identified and named the 'monomyth' in 1949. The quest underlies just about every form of storytelling, from religious myth to Greek epic to Hollywood blockbuster to personal memoir. In this structure, a protagonist is shaken out of his normal way of life by some disturbance and – often reluctantly at first, but at the urging of some kind of mentor or wise figure – strikes out on a journey to an unfamiliar realm. There he faces tests, battles enemies, questions the loyalty of friends and allies, withstands a climactic ordeal, teeters on the brink of failure or death, and ultimately returns to where he began, victorious but in some way transformed.[37]

Of course, many NDE stories are less intriguing and some – for instance, the frequent accounts of meetings with angels, or tall men in white robes – are disappointing (as every lapse from the imaginative into the *idées reçues* of orthodoxy is disappointing). Still, there are enough that are intriguing, uplifting and, tonally at least, rather inspiring, to make this hobby of mine rewarding. What may be the most intriguing feature of all is how NDEs transform their subjects' day to day lives, as Susan Blackmore points out:

> In the end it is probably a matter of personal preference whether to interpret the NDE as a glimpse of the life beyond or the product of the dying brain. Either way the NDE deserves serious research; and the dying, the recovering and their relatives deserve to know what we have learned ... Just as NDEs reduce the fear of death in the people who have them, so they can help all of us to accept death as a positive aspect of life. Indeed, the study of life at its

37 Gideon Lichfield, 'The Science of Near-Death Experiences', The Atlantic, April 2015

last limits may tell us more about ourselves and our lives than it does about death.

I believe that any NDE can be a valuable experience and, like Blackmore and others, I think this phenomenon should be investigated further. There is something inspirational about many near-death accounts – and even though my sojourn in the Red Zone does not conform to the classic NDE paradigm, (I did not leave my body, I did not pass beyond the white light that, for a moment, flooded my brain) I have to confess that I feel changed by the experience. Changed – permanently. I am not a 'better person' and I have not acquired the smallest measure of Zenlike wisdom. I do feel more appreciative, however. I stop and take note more than I have done for years. I am blessed with a fugitive sense of Blossomiest Blossom.

Still, having said all this, and at the risk of repeating myself, it seems necessary to say again that to be inspired by these accounts does not entail being convinced by them. I have never heard or read a near-death account that can be taken as proof of anything at all, whether it be the confirmation of some orthodox religious narrative or the sub-scientific 'fact' that, now and at the hour of our death, all human experience is 'just' a mere swirl of enzymes – or that the brain-mind complex is simply a one-way street. Anyone who has ever been alive for more than seven minutes knows that this pseudo-scientific 'explanation' is simplistic: to say that all experience is 'caused' by the fizz and slop of hormones through my brain is like saying that the exhilaration I used to get – *mea culpa* – from night-driving at high-speed on the old, sparsely policed M40 is 'caused' by a mix of motor oil and gasoline.

So, while speculation is always enjoyable, we are unable, as yet, to explain the NDE, much less explain it away. All we can say for sure is that we live, and we die, and life continues, by any means necessary. Individually, we make space for those who are still to come – after all, mortality is how we share the world – but the fact that a temporary ending will occasionally afford a little glimpse of halcyon is by no means evidence that we all come fitted with a tiny chip of immortality. Maybe, at the end, we sense some kind of continuity to life, but why make it personal? As a child, I was told that I possessed a soul, something that, though it may have been rented from God, was mine alone – but even as a first communion boy in white shorts and bowtie, I never took that idea with anything but a pinch of salt. Where did this mysterious entity reside? Was it lodged in the brain, or one of the body's more esoteric glands, as Classical anatomists once speculated? If there was anything in nature that corresponded to this soul, I could not imagine it as personal, try as I might – and, ironically, an early paradox that arose from my strictly Catholic education confirmed my suspicions for good. That this paradox was not obvious to the nuns, priests, and others of the faithful who taught me came as a surprise, since it was obvious enough that my twelve-year-old self could see it. Put simply, that paradox goes as follows:

a) in Latin, the word for soul is *anima*, which is the etymological root of animal, meaning a creature that is charged with life, a living thing – and yet:

b) in orthodox ideas of the afterlife, animals cannot go to heaven, for heaven is the reserve of human beings, who have a soul (while animals, apparently do not)

Ergo (my child mind reasoned) that which animates us, that which gives us life, is the soul and, at the same time, the one quality that we have in common with all other living things is the quality of being animate, of being *present* in a way that a rock is not. And yet, according to dogma, the very quality that we have in common with the other animals is the very thing that marks us out as different from (and, of course, superior to) them. Animals are animate, like us, but they are also soulless, meaning that they lack *anima*. This seemed a stretch, to say the least – though, of course, I had been too Jesuitically raised to abandon the idea of the soul altogether. There was a period of confusion, naturally, but it did not take long for me to conclude that, if there was 'soul', if it existed in some form, it belonged to the world, not to the person. After all, had not St Paul himself declared[38] that God is 'no respecter of persons'? Individual instances of life might share, for a time, in the force that through the green fuse drives the flower, but the natural order demands that they pass away to make room for new instances. Life is predicated on loss, continuity of the whole on individual mortality. Yet, when I dared to voice such thoughts, I was threatened with damnation by several of my teachers, while the more thoughtful divided into two, seemingly more considerate, groups – each of them sinister in its own way. In the blue corner, the party of older means wiser suggested that the phase I was going through was developmental and fairly common, and that I would, in due course 'return' to the blessed condition of simple faith. Meanwhile, the red corner regarded me with genuine pity and resolved to pray for my immortal soul (the one I had just declared non-existent). Such kindliness only confused me further. After all, the world was full of wicked people, with bad ideas; might I not have fallen into one of the traps that the wicked apparently delighted in preparing for the faithful? (Though I often wondered why they had nothing better to do.) It was a long time before I began to entertain the thought that, more by luck than judgment, I had only to take one small step to escape this legitimised, tax-exempt cult. It took even longer to acknowledge that, in all those Scripture classes of

38 Romans 2:11

my Catholic childhood (lessons in unreal thinking that were timetabled alongside, and were never categorised as distinct from, mathematics, or geography) I had become more and more alarmed at the thought of being *me* for all eternity. Had I been Gregory Peck, say, or James Clark Maxwell, it might have been closer to tolerable, but *me*? That seemed highly unfair – especially since, according to the orthodoxy, this *me* was condemned to dwell forever in a heavenly void of horses and timber wolves and birds (especially birds). At twelve, I could think of nothing worse. Or nothing, that is, other than Hell – and I was already fairly certain that, God being so kindly and merciful and everything, all that gleeful talk of the fiery furnace was a cautionary fib.

By now, it might seem that all this religious reminiscing has nothing to do with the subject at hand, and none of it is in any way unique – for too many of us, and certainly for most Catholic folk of my generation, such experiences are painfully familiar. Why our education system would saddle its children with arcane theological problems when they already have quadratic equations and puberty to deal with, I cannot say. Yet at the same time, I cannot help thinking that there is a real connection between orthodox religious ideas and extinction. For, just as so many of us, having been convinced of a life to come, squander the one life we are given in gogetting, petty squabbles and trivial pursuits, so, as a society, we have for centuries been busy squandering the only world we have on the understanding that there is another, more permanent and equitable kingdom somewhere in the ether. Even now, when we claim to be a secular society, we still live by the old monotheistic and otherworldly assumptions – assumptions that permeate even our scientific thinking. The analogy might be with a crumpled reveller on the first sober morning after a very long party: we are not drunk any more, but we do have one hell of a hangover. This is not to say that every corporate hack and politician-for-hire is a true believer (in heaven, or anything else), but it is the case that our thinking is still underpinned by the least appealing leftovers of religious dogma. We continue, as a society, to believe that, God-given or not, this world belongs to us. At the same time, this world is transitory and rife with original sin, and the only available consolation is the promise that Heaven – or, in more secular terms, The Future – is our final destination. Amidst all of creation, we believe that we are the only ones who are truly here – touched with God's love, or self-aware, or possessed of intellect, or whatever – and so the whole show belongs to us. That sense of entitlement is as obscene as it is embarrassing in its philosophical naiveté but, more than anything else, it is the main driver in our push towards the mass extinction that Barbara Ehrenreich finds us preparing for ourselves. At times, when we consider our wastefulness as a species, it is tempting to think that mass extinction is no more or less than we deserve. To accept that premise, however, is to accept that *Homo sapiens* is defined by its greediest and least thoughtful class. For now, with no illusions as to how far such a position can be justified, I choose to cling to the notion that humanity as a whole is telling a story that is more interesting than that – a story in which soul may well figure, though if it does, it is unlikely to be personal.

If Kierkegaard is right, and self sits at the point of play between the finite and the infinite, then it might be useful to distinguish, if only for myself, between that aspect of self's synthesis that is contingent, societally defined and of fixed abode – the 'person', that is, of which St Paul's God is no respecter – and the self that is aligned with the infinite. Seen from the side of finitude, 'I' is an instance, a person with *this* name, *this* face, defined by *these* personal and cultural characteristics, but when 'I' is perceived in its infinite aspect, *sub specie aeternitatis*, it is no longer limited by circumstance, a thread of psyche freed, in Jung's words, from the illusions of time and space, no longer singular and yet, not plural, one with the fabric of the Overall. If this should be the case, then the death of an individual instance is a loss only in the contingent sense – an absence, for those left behind, in time and space – and the justice of its passing becomes apparent. As has been said, this is how we share the world. The birth and life and death of instances is evidence of the constant flux of temporal being, and one thing makes way for another, *ad infinitum*. 'From my rotting body, flowers shall grow, and I am in them and that is eternity,' says Edvard Munch. Seen from this perspective, the individual instance partakes of soul to the extent that it is animated by something infinite, but it *possesses* nothing. Soul is impersonal. Yet, just as there are two ways of thinking about the self (which can be pictured as existing on a sliding scale between finite and infinite, so to speak) so there are two terms for soul: *anima*, and *alma*. This is a thorny subject, from a philosophical point of view, but for the purposes of this entirely speculative enquiry, it might be interesting to think of *anima* as that borrowed soul seen in the living instance – the élan *vital* that animates each live thing – while considering *alma* as an attribute of the species as a whole, the force that makes a species what it is, *sui generis*, distinct from all others and irreplaceable. Taking this view, we can see the loss of an instance as a natural event, part of the flux of incarnation, while the loss of a species is a terrible, bleak *cul de sac*. Instances echo down bloodlines, a dead woman will appear, momentarily, in the smile or the laugh of a great-granddaughter, say; but when a species becomes extinct, that form is gone: no echoes, no shadow, no living memory. More: it is gone, not only as itself, but as the part it played in the Overall, so that every remaining creature for which it was once an Other is condemned to live without it, in a diminished world – and as the extinctions multiply, so the world becomes more and more impoverished, the fabric of life more and more threadbare. This is the source of our grief, and it is this – our greatest moral crisis *as a species* – that we should be doing everything in our power to resolve.

It's that time of the afternoon when everything seems far away – the rooks in the beech trees at the end of my paddock, a cow bellowing in a far field – a moment in the middle of the day when I have the sense that something here, something invisible to the human eye, is remembering the time before humanity arrived. The time before, when there was no trace on the air of diesel or deodorant or Kentucky Fried Chicken. No traffic noise down on the coast road, where the boys are racing home from work, no sudden glare of headlamps coming up the hill in the cold gloaming. I linger on that thought: once upon a time, I was not here, the world was happening without me. The small parcel of meadow where I now stand once extended from the ridge at my back to the edge of the sea, the wind blew across this land unimpeded by my house or my little garden studio. I feel humbled by this thought, but I do not feel diminished. I do not feel small, or large, or anything more or less than the thinking meat that I am, fortunate to have been born into a live world, even as I am aware that I will, in the not-so-distant future, die out of it. In spite of my Catholic schooling, I am inclined to believe that, individually, as one instance of a particularly troublesome, yet curiously inventive species, my exit will be final. An ending. At the same time, I have the sense that something will carry on – though whatever that something is, I do not think that it will be personal. A stray thread of the force that through the green fuse drives the flower, a nugget of electricity, a scrap of the universal Id, a pulse that is not located in one place or another but dwells everywhere – nothing I can say even begins to define this something, but that is because the instance that I am dwells here, in this place, at this point in history. Indeed, even in those moments when I can hold two conflicting ideas in my head at once, and as much as I know that, in the Dreamtime, stories do not begin and end, I must accept that, when we tell them here, we have to shape them to linear time, because that is how we narrate the here and now to one another. Also, when I say that, in the Dreaming, in the realm of once upon a time, everything happens at once, when I make the counter-intuitive claim that time is not linear, when I insist that everything is now, there will be those who think that all this is just mumbo-jumbo, metaphysics, a wishful feast of New Age nonsense. I could say that nothing is further from the truth, that I am as down-to-earth a human as anyone cursed with the habit of speculation could be, but the truth is, I don't really care. What I care about is what is happening here, on Earth. At the level of instance, what is happening to me, now, is fine. The odd, though perhaps not that surprising thing about any brush with mortality is that, afterwards, should you survive, everything seems more precious, more vivid. A localised but not altogether personal attention seems to linger on the day-to-day details, on the quiddity of things and the heart, in the words of Kamala Harris' Covid Monument speech, tends to cherish the simple moments. In short, to extend the run of clichés here, I feel blessed. More alive, less impatient and altogether ready for what is to come. At the same time, I grieve for every extinction, past, present and future, not just because I have children (though that is part of it) but also because I would rather not imagine a world so diminished by any further loss of species and places and cultures. I like this planet. I like animals, birds in particular. I like gingkoes and geckos and I particularly like giraffes. I like ferns of every kind, fire-bellied toads and flamingos. I can think of few things as beautiful as the song of the Western Meadowlark. I would very much like these things to continue.

For now, though, I have enough. It is winter on a not particularly scenic hilltop in Central Scotland, but what there is – it comes to me again – is a manifestation of the common miracle. Incarnation. The unscripted and ungraspable Overall. As the light starts to wane, greylag and pink-footed geese descend on the fields around me, dusk setting in as they dip down out of the sky so that all I have is the music, the sudden beating of wings and wild calls in the half-dark and that vague sense of a larger presence, a presence that we have thinned and diminished, but have not expunged – testament to the stubbornness of a life that will persist beyond us, blossoming in the ruins of all that we build and abandon and, should humanity come to some kind of ending, moving on, new species by new, unpredictable species, till every trace of this perverse and self-destructive civilisation is gone.

IN THE COUNTRY *Kenneth Allsop*
THROUGH THE WOODS *H. E. Bates*
MEN AND THE FIELDS *Adrian Bell*
AUROCHS AND AUKS *John Burnside*
ORISON FOR A CURLEW *Horatio Clare*
SOMETHING OF HIS ART: WALKING WITH J. S. BACH *Horatio Clare*
ARBOREAL: WOODLAND WORDS *Adrian Cooper*
ISLAND YEARS, ISLAND FARM *Frank Fraser Darling*
LANDFILL *Tim Dee*
HERBACEOUS *Paul Evans*
THE PATTERN UNDER THE PLOUGH *George Ewart Evans*
THE SCREAMING SKY *Charles Foster*
THE TREE *John Fowles*
AN ENGLISH FARMHOUSE *Geoffrey Grigson*
TIME AND PLACE *Alexandra Harris*
MADE IN ENGLAND *Dorothy Hartley*
THE MAKING OF THE ENGLISH LANDSCAPE *W. G. Hoskins*
A SHEPHERD'S LIFE *W. H. Hudson*
WILD LIFE IN A SOUTHERN COUNTY *Richard Jefferies*
FOUR HEDGES *Clare Leighton*
DREAM ISLAND *R. M. Lockley*
THE UNOFFICIAL COUNTRYSIDE *Richard Mabey*
EMPERORS, ADMIRALS AND CHIMNEY SWEEPERS *Peter Marren*
RING OF BRIGHT WATER *Gavin Maxwell*
DIARY OF A YOUNG NATURALIST *Dara McAnulty*
WHERE? *Simon Moreton*
COPSFORD *Walter Murray*
LOVE, MADNESS, FISHING *Dexter Petley*
THE LONG FIELD *Pamela Petro*
SHALIMAR *Davina Quinlivan*
THE ASH TREE *Oliver Rackham*
ANCIENT WOODS OF THE HELFORD RIVER *Oliver Rackham*
LIMESTONE COUNTRY *Fiona Sampson*
MY HOUSE OF SKY: THE LIFE OF J. A. BAKER *Hetty Saunders*
SNOW *Marcus Sedgwick*
WATER AND SKY, RIDGE AND FURROW *Neil Sentance*
BLACK APPLES OF GOWER *Iain Sinclair*
THE FAT OF THE LAND *John Seymour*
BEYOND THE FELL WALL *Richard Skelton*
CORNERSTONES: SUBTERRANEAN WRITING *Mark Smalley*
IN PURSUIT OF SPRING *Edward Thomas*
ON SILBURY HILL *Adam Thorpe*
THE NATURAL HISTORY OF SELBORNE *Gilbert White*
NO MATTER HOW MANY SKIES HAVE FALLEN *Ken Worpole*
KING OF DUST *Alex Woodcock*
GHOST TOWN: A LIVERPOOL SHADOWPLAY *Jeff Young*

Little Toller Books
w. littletoller.co.uk   e. books@littletoller.co.uk